Beginning Bazel

Building and Testing for Java, Go, and More

P.J. McNerney

Apress®

Beginning Bazel: Building and Testing for Java, Go, and More

P.J. McNerney
Blackhawk, CO, USA

ISBN-13 (pbk): 978-1-4842-5193-5   ISBN-13 (electronic): 978-1-4842-5194-2
https://doi.org/10.1007/978-1-4842-5194-2

Managing Director, Apress Media LLC: Welmoed Spahr
Acquisitions Editor: Steve Anglin
Development Editor: Matthew Moodie
Editorial Operations Manager: Mark Powers

Cover designed by eStudioCalamar

Cover image designed by Raw Pixel (www.rawpixel.com)

Distributed to the book trade worldwide by Springer Science+Business Media New York, 233 Spring Street, 6th Floor, New York, NY 10013. Phone 1-800-SPRINGER, fax (201) 348-4505, e-mail orders-ny@springer-sbm.com, or visit www.springeronline.com. Apress Media, LLC is a California LLC and the sole member (owner) is Springer Science + Business Media Finance Inc (SSBM Finance Inc). SSBM Finance Inc is a **Delaware** corporation.

For information on translations, please e-mail editorial@apress.com; for reprint, paperback, or audio rights, please email bookpermissions@springernature.com.

Apress titles may be purchased in bulk for academic, corporate, or promotional use. eBook versions and licenses are also available for most titles. For more information, reference our Print and eBook Bulk Sales web page at http://www.apress.com/bulk-sales.

Any source code or other supplementary material referenced by the author in this book is available to readers on GitHub via the book's product page, located at www.apress.com/9781484251935. For more detailed information, please visit http://www.apress.com/source-code.

Printed on acid-free paper

Table of Contents

About the Author

P.J. McNerney is a developer with over 20 years experience as a software engineer, having worked for a variety of companies, including Google, DreamWorks Animation, Insomniac Games, Goldman Sachs, and Major League Baseball. He lives in Colorado with beloved wife, children, and their dogs.

About the Technical Reviewer

Laurent LeBrun is a software engineer at Google in Munich. He has been working with Bazel since 2011 and helped open-source it in 2015. He led the design and implementation of Starlark, to provide an extension mechanism to Bazel.

In the past, he has worked on a contract basis with Microsoft using the F# language. In his free time, he creates real time 3D animations as part of the demo scene.

CHAPTER 1

Introduction

Welcome to the world of Bazel!

In case you haven't heard about it, Bazel is the open source version of the build system used at Google (Alphabet). To give a sense of scale, Bazel was designed to solve some of the core problems of building at Google, namely, having to build literally *millions* of lines of code across a multitude of languages, efficiently and correctly, for multiple platforms (e.g., server, mobile, desktop) and different hardware architectures.

While the build system was initially internal to Google, it was released to open source a few years ago. Since that time, it has continued to evolve into a high-performance, powerful, yet simple build system for production-level needs.

What This Book Is

Beginning Bazel is meant as a gentle and practical introduction into using the Bazel build system. As you progress through the book, you will learn the basics of Bazel through a series of targeted examples.

These examples are aimed at teaching the core concepts and constructs of Bazel, including how to set up some basic build targets, construct and cultivate your workspace to pull in new language rules, and easily build both command line and mobile applications within the same project across multiple languages.

Through the course of this book, you will build examples in various languages, tying them together in a cohesive fashion and generating working binaries that could run on a server and on mobile (with examples covering both Android and iOS).

What This Book Is Not

Beginning Bazel is not a comprehensive reference manual. While you will learn some of the core commands for Bazel, there are *many* options and avenues that are not covered

1

© P.J. McNerney 2020
P.J. McNerney, *Beginning Bazel*, https://doi.org/10.1007/978-1-4842-5194-2_1

in this book (perhaps a future sequel will explore some of the areas). Fortunately, Bazel's documentation is excellent: `https://docs.bazel.build`. This has the information on latest and greatest advancements happening for Bazel.

Also, while Bazel is able to build most languages, this text only covers a very small fraction of them. Fortunately, the patterns that you will learn in this book are applicable across most of the languages that you are likely to encounter and use with Bazel.

New language rules are popping up all the time, so it is worthwhile to check out the main GitHub organization at `https://github.com/bazelbuild`. Additionally, Awesome Bazel (`www.awesomebazel.com`) is a great site for a curated set of Bazel rules and very worthwhile to check out to see some fun new possibilities for the language.

Features of Bazel

One of the chief goals of Bazel is to make sure that your builds are hermetic, that is, that the build dependencies (including both dependent libraries and build tools) are well known and independent of anything that may or may not be installed on any given machine. Ideally, any build can be reproduced using only the tools within the given project's workspace.

To this end, Bazel takes special care to ensure that you are explicitly specifying all of your dependencies and eschewing any "magic" in creating your build. Some might object that this is removing a degree of convenience. However, in reality this explicit specification allows both Bazel and the user to reason intelligently about the builds and provide tools to help diagnose and fix issues as they occur.

Bazel has many features that make it attractive as a build system:

- High-level, extensible build language

- Explicit dependency management

- Advanced visibility rules

- Explicit workspace management

- Remote build execution and caching

- Build dependency analysis

- Fast, correct builds

High-Level Build Language

Bazel provides a very simple yet powerful set of constructs. These include (but are not limited to)

- Commands (such as *build* and *test*)

- Rules (e.g., for handling different languages)

- Packages (to collate a set of rules and dependencies together)

- Workspaces (to define the working files, outputs, and dependencies of your project)

Additionally, Starlark (formerly Skylark) is Bazel's build language (inspired by Python). Starlark can further extend Bazel to create new language rules, macros to assist in development, and so on.

Explicit Dependency Management

As previously mentioned, Bazel requires explicit dependency declaration. There is no proverbial "free lunch" with Bazel as it favors being explicit over any kind of implicit "magic" (e.g., the location of the header files in C++). When creating a build target (e.g., a library), you are required to specify each of the files (or some directive collating all of the files); if you don't specify it, Bazel will not see it.

Additionally, as you depend upon other targets (e.g., another library), this dependency must be defined explicitly; otherwise, your build will likely fail. In the limit, this explicit declaration of dependencies from one target to another forms a directed dependency graph.

Finally, the directed dependency graph in Bazel is and always must be a *directed acyclic graph.* That is, there are no cycles allowed within a Bazel dependency graph. This is important when attempting to create coherent builds, since cycles in the build tree imply the need for some kind of heuristic to break the cycle (or let the cycle break the build). Attempting to create a cycle within a dependency graph and then build against it will immediately cause Bazel to break the build and warn you of the error.

Advanced Visibility Features

One of the best features of Bazel is the ability to limit the visibility of your packages and targets. That is, you can effectively reduce the scope of what packages can actually depend upon your build targets. While similar features exist in languages like Java (i.e., package visibility) and C++ (i.e., namespaces), Bazel creates the ability to constrain visibility of dependencies to any language.

Explicit Workspace Management

Similar to dependency graph management, Bazel also gives you the ability to fully specify the dependencies of your workspace on any other dependencies, including external repos. This gives you the ability to pull in code, files, and so on from other sources, often through specific versions of the external dependencies. This helps provide guarantees of correctness while still giving you flexibility.

Remote Build Execution and Caching

Although Bazel executes locally by default, Bazel also allows you to set up a distributed build system with intelligent caching. This capability is incredibly useful for speeding up individual builds as well as helping to accelerate development across an entire team.

Build Dependency Analysis

Another powerful feature is the ability to analyze a build target's dependencies. For anyone who has ever tried to introspect into a build product and asked, "How did *that* get in there?" Bazel's ability to understand a build target's dependency graph will come as a welcome tool. This is incredibly useful for simplifying dependencies, optimization, and so on.

Fast, Correct Builds (and Tests)

While all the other features are grand in their own right, together they help to provide the most important feature of all for Bazel: efficient and reliable builds (and, consequently, tests). At the end of the day, the purpose of a build system is to transform code and data into working applications in a speedy and correct fashion.

Bazel utilizes its many features to create a coherent and optimized method of building products. In addition, it has an intelligent caching system to ensure that rebuilding (since development is mostly all about rebuilding) is quick and correct, with little need for cleaning.

When all is said and done, the best feature of Bazel is that it works quickly, simply, and correctly. You can put together a simple Bazel project, execute it, and then easily extend it over time.

Who This Book Is For (and Possibly Not For)

Beginning Bazel is aimed at introducing Bazel to everyone. The degree of utility you get out of Bazel, however, will largely be determined by what kinds of problems you are trying to solve.

As indicated at the beginning of this chapter, Bazel was originally designed to solve the problems around efficiently and correctly building a massive code base for multiple languages, platforms, and architectures. However, Bazel also scales really nicely, from the simplest application to a full-stack set of microservices and mobile applications.

Indeed, Bazel may be most useful if you...

- ...are starting from scratch and want a build system that is going to scale with your needs

- ...want to coherently build and depend upon multiple languages

- ...want out-of-the-box support for defining and running tests

- ...want to easily build against multiple architectures

- ...want intelligent caching of build products

- ...want deterministic outputs every time you build

- ...want a production-level build system

- ...are willing to operate within the boundaries of Bazel

This last point may seem a bit strange; however, Bazel is an opinionated build system. In order to ensure the guarantees of speed and correctness, it will actively prevent you from doing counterproductive things (e.g., circular build dependencies). Additionally, Bazel operates best when it is the primary build system. While it *can* work with other build systems (although this is outside the scope of this book), you are going to maximize the power and utility of Bazel by using it everywhere in your project.

To that end, it is worthwhile to point out that Bazel might not be for everyone. In particular, you *might* not find that much utility in Bazel under the following situations:

- You are only dealing with a single language (e.g., Java, Kotlin) for a specific purpose (e.g., server-side programming, Android). In this case, you might find existing tools (e.g., Gradle) may be just fine for your needs.

- You have a single, small project that is focused only on a single architecture with limited requirements on additional libraries (e.g., programming for iOS). Again, you might find that existing tools (e.g., Xcode project) are fine.

- You are already happy with your existing build system.

On this last point, you may already have a perfectly good build system, in which case, Bazel may just be a curiosity.

Additionally, you may already be an expert in Bazel; in this case, this book may not provide that much utility for you (in which case, you might want to give it to a friend to share your love of Bazel).

However, for everyone else, you might have just found the best build system for your needs.

CHAPTER 2

Setup and Installation

Before we start building, we need to install Bazel and any other tools and frameworks required (e.g., compilers). In this chapter, we will demonstrate the necessary steps among several operating systems.

Note Throughout the course of this book, we will be using Bazel version 1.0.0. Bazel is evolving rapidly, with new capabilities and configurations coming all the time. In this evolution, there may be changes to the dependencies which require tweaks to the build code. For the sake of the examples here, it is best for you to normalize against version 1.0.0. Once you have gotten the hang of Bazel, you can upgrade to later versions and tweak the examples as necessary.

We will cover the installation instructions for the following operating systems: Windows, MacOS, and Ubuntu Linux. Additional installation instructions may be found at `https://docs.bazel.build/versions/master/install.html`.

Since we are focused on version 1.0.0 of Bazel, we can find the installation binaries required for all of our platforms at `https://github.com/bazelbuild/bazel/releases/`.

For all operating systems, we will need some basic tools in order to bootstrap Bazel. These include the tools and frameworks for building and running Python, Java, and C++. Although we *won't* be explicitly building any C++ projects in the course of this book, we will be depending upon projects which do build C++ (e.g., Protocol Buffers).

© P.J. McNerney 2020
P.J. McNerney, *Beginning Bazel*, https://doi.org/10.1007/978-1-4842-5194-2_2

Note   Java, Python, and C++ are "special" with regard to Bazel because they largely comprise the *built*-in languages whose rules come out of the box with Bazel. That is, the rules for building libraries and binary using these languages come as a part of Bazel itself.

Other languages that we will build over the course of this book are Go and Swift; however, we don't need to explicitly download tools for them. Instead, we will see that by virtue of depending upon external projects and registering the appropriate toolchains, we will get the components to build these languages for "free." There will be more on this in later chapters.

MacOS

Installing Xcode

For installation on MacOS, we will first need to install Xcode for performing the basic build actions. The simplest way to retrieve Xcode is to open the App Store application on MacOS and download the application.

Figure 2-1. *Retrieving Xcode from the App Store*

Once you have downloaded the application, you will need to open the application and accept the license agreement.

Alternatively, you can accept the license agreement on the command line. To do so, open a terminal window and execute the following:

```
~$ sudo xcodebuild -license accept
```

Installing Bazel

Once you have set up Xcode, you are now ready to install Bazel onto your machine. Download the Bazel binary installer for 1.0.0. This can be found at `https://github.com/bazelbuild/bazel/releases/download/1.0.0/bazel-1.0.0-installer-darwin-x86_64.sh`.

After this has downloaded, navigate to the directory (e.g., Downloads) to which you have downloaded the installation script. As a precaution, you may need to first ensure that you can execute the installation script by changing the file's permissions. Once done, you can then run installation.

```
~$ cd Downloads
~/Downloads$ chmod +x bazel-1.0.0-installer-darwin-x86_64.sh
~/Downloads$ ./bazel-1.0.0-installer-darwin-x86_64.sh –user
```

The *--user* flag installs Bazel to ~/bin (i.e., your user's *bin* directory). To ensure that you can run Bazel, make sure that ~/bin is in your default paths. Add the following to your ~/.zshrc (or .bashrc if you are using a version of MacOs earlier than Catalina) file.

```
export PATH="$PATH:$HOME/bin"
```

Once you have added this in, source your ~/.zshrc (or ~/.bashrc) file to make sure the new path is picked up.

```
~$ source ~/.zshrc
```

Now you are all set to run Bazel on MacOS. You can easily verify this on the command line using the *version* directive, which will output what version of Bazel you are using.

```
~$ bazel --version
bazel 1.0.0
```

Installing Java

You will need at least Java 8 for the examples presented in this book. For MacOS 10.7 and above, Java is no longer installed by default; instead, we need to explicitly download and install it.

Head over to `https://java.com/en/download/mac_download.jsp` to download Java. Once you have downloaded the file to your computer, follow the instructions to install Java on your computer.

Once you are done, open a terminal and verify that you have successfully installed Java on your computer by running the following:

```
~$ java -version
java version "1.8.0_181"
Java(TM) SE Runtime Environment (build 1.8.0_181-b13)
Java HotSpot(TM) 64-Bit Server VM (build 25.181-b13, mixed mode)java
```

Verifying Your Python Version

By default, Python comes packaged with your MacOS machine. You will need at least Python 2.7.15 in order to run the examples in this book. To verify that you have a sufficient version of Python on your computer, open a terminal to verify your version.

```
~$ python --version
Python 2.7.15
```

Note   At the time of this writing, both Python 2 and Python 3 work with Bazel, with a migration path currently in place to get to the latter. You *can* set your default to be one or the other; however, this is considered outside the scope of this book for the sake of the examples presented therein; currently they should work with either version.

Ubuntu Linux

Installing Required Packages

Installation on Ubuntu is very similar to MacOS. However, in this case, instead of downloading Xcode, we will be installing a set of required packages (i.e., pkg-config, zip, g++, zlib1g-dev, unzip, python3).

Open a terminal window and execute the following command:

```
~$ sudo apt-get install pkg-config zip g++ zlib1g-dev unzip python3
```

This may require you to install additional packages as well. Press "Y" when asked if additional packages should be installed.

Installing Bazel

Having retrieved the prerequisites, you are ready to download Bazel. Retrieve the installation script from https://github.com/bazelbuild/bazel/releases/download/1.0.0/bazel-1.0.0-installer-linux-x86_64.sh.

Open a terminal and navigate to the location where you downloaded the file (e.g., ~/.Downloads). It may be necessary to set the permissions to execute the file. After that is taken care of, you can run the execution.

```
~$ cd Downloads
~/Downloads$ chmod +x bazel-1.0.0-installer-linux-x86_64.sh
~/Downloads$ ./bazel-1.0.0-installer-linux-x86_64.sh --user
```

The *--user* flag installs Bazel to ~/bin (i.e., your user's *bin* directory). To ensure that you can run Bazel, make sure that ~/bin is in your default paths. Add the following to your ~/.bashrc file:

```
export PATH="$PATH:$HOME/bin"
```

Once you have added this in, source your *~/.bashrc* file to make sure the new path is picked up.

```
~$ source ~/.bashrc
```

Now you are all set to run Bazel on Ubuntu. You can easily verify this on the command line using the *version* directive, which will output what version of Bazel you are using.

```
~$ bazel --version
bazel 1.0.0
```

Installing Java

To ensure that we are installing the correct version of Java (via OpenJDK), we first need to check your version of Ubuntu. Open a terminal and execute the following:

```
~$ lsb_release -a
No LSB modules area available
Distributor ID: Ubuntu
Description:        Ubuntu 16.04.5 LTS
Release:           16.04
Codename:          xenial
```

If you are using Ubuntu 16.04, then you will need to use OpenJDK 8. Run the following command line:

```
~$ sudo apt-get install openjdk-8-jdk
```

If you are using Ubuntu 18.04, then you will need to use Open JDK 11. Run the following command line instead:

```
~$ sudo apt-get install openjdk-11-jdk
```

In each case, it may be necessary to install additional packages in order to complete the Java installation.

After you are done with installation, verify the version of Java you have installed by running the following:

```
~$ java -version
openjdk version "1.8.0_222"
OpenJDK Runtime Environment (build 1.8.0_222-8u222-b10-
1ubuntu1~16.04.1-b10)
OpenJDK 64-Bit Server VM (build 25.222-b10, mixed mode)
```

Windows

Setting Up Your System

In order to use Bazel, it is recommended that you have 64-bit Windows 10, version 1703 or above. To check your Windows version, open *Settings*.

Figure 2-2. *Windows Settings*

Select *System* ➤ *About*. The information you need is under *Windows Specification*.

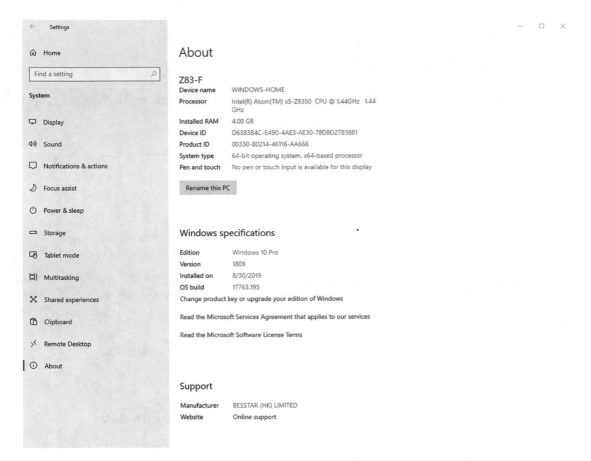

Figure 2-3. *Verifying the OS build of Windows*

Additionally, you will need to enable Developer Mode in order to develop on your machine. Go to *Settings* ➤ *Update & Security* ➤ *For developers.*

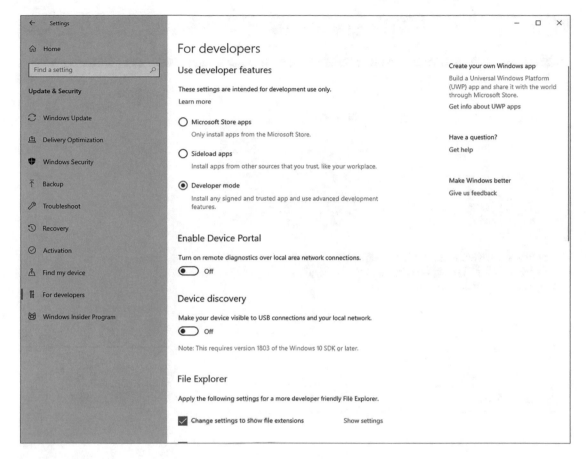

Figure 2-4. *Enabling Developer Mode*

Under *Use developer features*, select *Developer mode*. It may be necessary to wait for the Developer package to be downloaded.

Installing Required Applications

You will need several applications prior to actually retrieving Bazel itself.

Visual C++ Redistributable for Visual Studio 2015

This package contains the runtime components required for executing C++ applications built using Visual Studio 2015. Navigate to www.microsoft.com/en-us/download/ developer-tools.aspx and search for *Visual C++ Redistributable for Visual Studio 2015*.

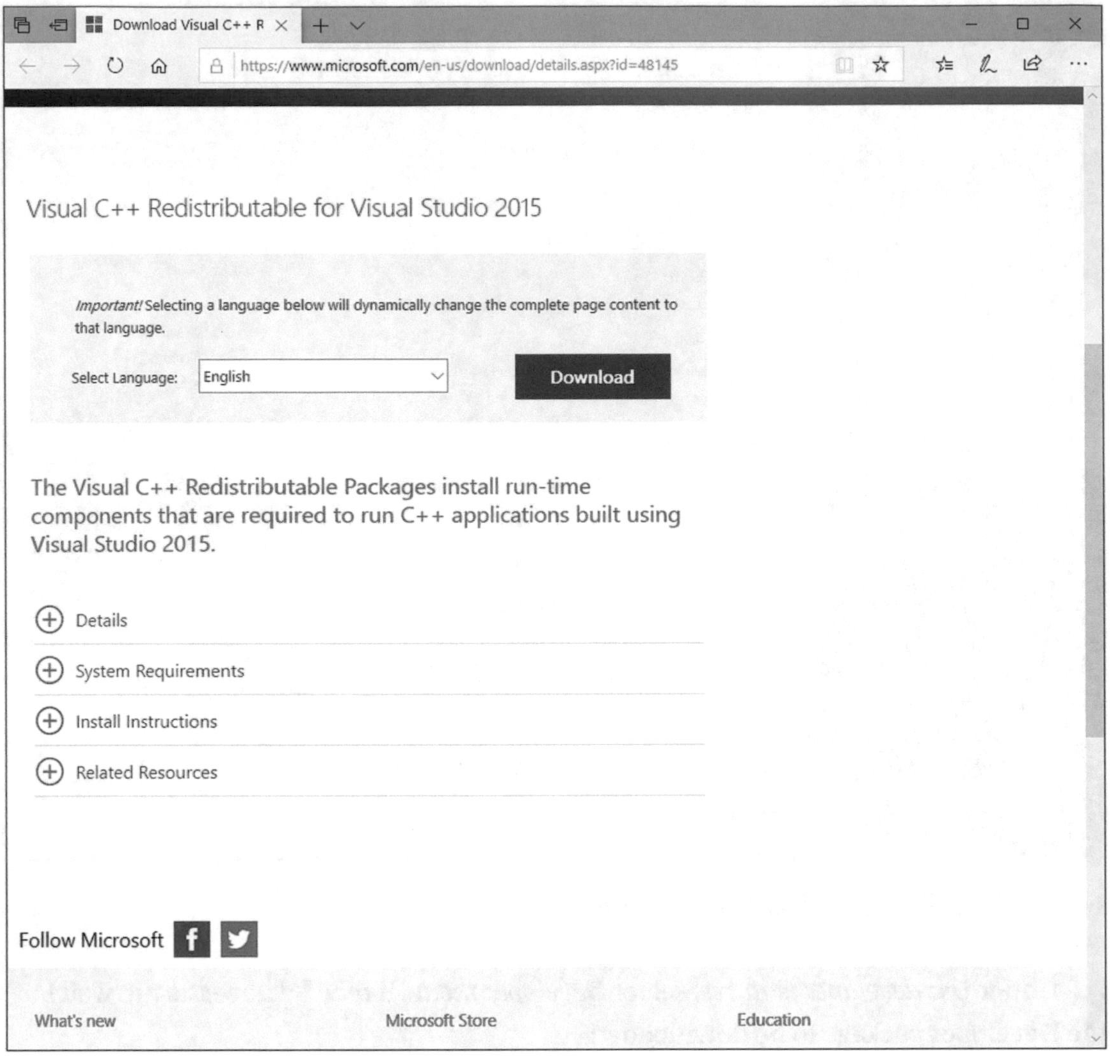

Figure 2-5. *Retrieving the Visual C++ Redistributable Packages*

Download the package and install it on your computer.

MSYS2

MSYS2 is a platform that provides some basic tools for software distribution and building; in this context, we will be most interested in the fact that it provides a bash shell for Windows. It also provides a package management system to make it easy to install software, similar to what might be seen in Linux (e.g., through *apt-get*) or MacOS (e.g., through something like *Homebrew*).

Navigate to `www.msys2.org/` and download MSYS2 for x86_64. Install the software on your computer; for simplicity, use the default installation path.

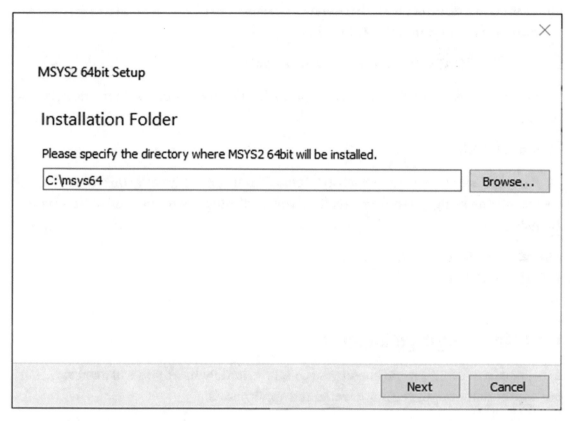

Figure 2-6. Installing MSYS2 to your computer

Once you have completed installation, open an MSYS2 terminal. You will need to install several packages (i.e., *zip*, *unzip*, *patch*, *diffutils*, and *git*). Execute the following command within the terminal:

```
pjmcn@WINDOWS-HOME MSYS~
$ pacman -S zip unzip patch diffutils git
```

You may need to install additional packages in order to complete the installations.

Bazel Installation

Having taken care of the necessary components, you are now ready to download and install Bazel itself. Retrieve the executable from `https://github.com/bazelbuild/bazel/releases/download/1.0.0/bazel-1.0.0-windows-x86_64.exe`.

Unlike Linux and MacOS, the downloaded executable *is* the Bazel executable; there is no separate installation script. Once you have downloaded the application, move the application to a directory (e.g., C:\Users\<user name>\bin) and rename it to *bazel.exe*.

Add the path to your MSYS2 *.bashrc* file.

```
export PATH="$PATH:/c/Users/<username>/bin"
```

Once you have added this in, source your ~/.*bashrc* file to make sure the new path is picked up.

```
~$ source ~/.bashrc
```

Now you are all set to run Bazel on Windows. You can easily verify this on the command line using the *version* directive, which will output what version of Bazel you are using.

```
pjmcn@WINDOWS-HOME MSYS~
$ bazel --version
bazel 1.0.0
```

Installing Language Support

In order to work with several languages (C++, Java, and Python), you will need to install the appropriate supporting frameworks and applications.

C++

Although we will not be directly building C++ applications within this book, there are several libraries upon which we will depend which require C++ support. Navigate to https://visualstudio.microsoft.com/downloads/#build-tools-for-visual-studio-2019. Download the Build Tools Installer and run the installation.

Figure 2-7. *Retrieving the Build Tools for Visual Studio 2019*

During the course of installation, make sure you select the C++ build tools.

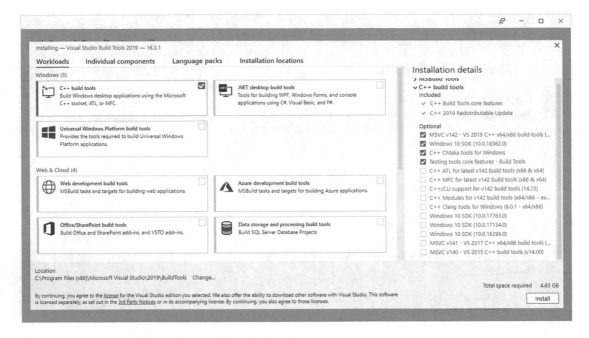

Figure 2-8. *Installing the C++ build tools*

Java

Many examples in this book do use Java. Navigate to www.oracle.com/technetwork/
java/javase/downloads/index.html. You will need to download at least Java SE
Development Kit 10 for Windows x64. Download an appropriate installation executable
and install it on your computer.

Note   MSYS2 has difficulty with spaces within paths. The default path places
Java into *Program Files*. In order to avoid any issues, you should change your
installation path to someplace without spaces (e.g., C:\Users\<user name>\bin\
Java\<jdk-version>\).

As you did with Bazel, make sure to add in the path to your Java installation into the
PATH of your bash shell within your *.bashrc* file.

```
export PATH="$PATH:/c/Users/<user name>/bin/Java/<jdk-version>/bin"
```

Additionally, you will need to also set your *JAVA_HOME* variable.

```
export JAVA_HOME="/c/Users/<user name>/bin/Java/<jdk-version>"
```

Source the *.bashrc* and confirm that Java is all set within MSYS2.

```
pjmcn@WINDOWS-HOME MSYS~
$ source .bashrc
pjmcn@WINDOWS-HOME MSYS~
$ java --version
java version "11.0.4" 2019-07-16 LTS
Java™ SE Runtime Environment 18.9 (build 11.0.4+10-LTS)
Java Hotspot™ 64-Bit Server VM 18.9 (build 11.0.4+10-LTS, mixed mode)
```

Python

Finally, in order to build for Python, you will need to download either Python 2.7 or 3 for Windows. Navigate to `www.python.org/downloads/release/python-2716` and download the Windows x86-64 MSI Installer. After you have downloaded the installer, execute it in order to install Python.

Once again, make sure you add the path to Python into the PATH of your bash shell.

```
export PATH="$PATH:/c/Python27"
```

Source the .bashrc and confirm that python is all set within MSYS2.

```
pjmcn@WINDOWS-HOME MSYS~
$ source .bashrc
pjmcn@WINDOWS-HOME MSYS~
$ python --version
Python 2.7.16
```

Final Word

At this stage, you should be able to execute the Bazel examples within this book. For additional operating systems that you may want to install Bazel on, navigate to `https://docs.bazel.build/versions/master/install.html`.

Having taken care of the scaffolding necessary to run Bazel, you are now ready to jump in and start having some fun.

CHAPTER 3

Your First Bazel Project

Now that you've downloaded and set up Bazel, the real fun begins. We'll start with a small project just to get started and then build (no pun intended) from there.

By the end of this chapter, you will have your first Bazel project up and running and be able to build and test code.

Setting Up Your Workspace

Prior to adding any code, we establish a new Bazel project by creating a WORKSPACE file to a given directory.

Create a directory for your project and create an empty WORKSPACE file:

```
$ mkdir chapter_03 (or <name of your directory>)
$ cd chapter_03 (or <name of your directory>)
chapter_03$ touch WORKSPACE
```

The location of the WORKSPACE file should always be at the root of your Bazel project. Within your Bazel project, all paths will be relativized to the WORKSPACE file. As you create your various build targets in various directories, you will be able to refer to them relative to the WORKSPACE file.

However, this is just the tip of the iceberg of the powers of the WORKSPACE file. Later on, we will see how to use the WORKSPACE file to

- Add new remote code repositories to your workspace (which you can then refer to later on)

- Add new rules for compiling in different languages

For now, however, the empty WORKSPACE file alone gives us a lot to work with, so we will start from there.

© P.J. McNerney 2020
P.J. McNerney, *Beginning Bazel*, https://doi.org/10.1007/978-1-4842-5194-2_3

Adding Source Code

While the WORKSPACE file defines the root of your Bazel project, you will define a source directory (possibly multiple source directories) into which to place your code. Code organization is one reason for this, since you will want to have some kind of structure.

However, there is at least one more good reason: Bazel is going to create new sub-directories in the same location as your WORKSPACE directory. We will get into the particulars of these directories shortly, since they pertain to the build products that come out of the Bazel build processes.

Create a directory for your source code:

```
chapter_03$ mkdir src (or your favorite directory name)
```

Caution   When considering what to call your directory, do not use one of the following names:

- `bazel-bin`
- `bazel-out`
- `bazel-testlogs`
- `bazel-chapter_03` (or `bazel-<name of your directory>`)

If you haven't guessed yet, these are the special directories that Bazel creates. Creating a directory that aliases with one of these is asking for trouble, so please save yourself a lot of headache by just picking a different name (like `src`). Also, while the preceding directories are indicative of the current version of Bazel, it is advisable to avoid any directories following a pattern of "bazel-*".

Hello World, Java Style

Out of the box (at the time of this writing), Bazel supports C++, Java, and Python without any additional configuration. To start, we will create a (slightly modified) Java version of Hello World. (Don't worry. We'll get more complex; this is just to get started.)

In your preferred code editor, create the file `HelloWorld.java` and write the following.

Listing 3-1. A simple Java program

```
public class HelloWorld {
  public static void main(String[] args) {
    System.out.println("Hello, World!);
  }
}
```

Save that file to disk, under your src directory.

Specifying the BUILD Targets

With the code created, we can now turn our attention to the basic Bazel components required to actually build your work.

Within your src directory, create the file BUILD and write and save the following.

Listing 3-2. Your first BUILD file

```
java_binary(
    name = "HelloWorld",
    srcs = ["HelloWorld.java"],
)
```

In this example, HelloWorld is a *build target*; that is, HelloWorld is a unit that can be identified and built.

Building Your Targets

Having defined something to build, we are now ready to actually build it. Before we do, however, let's jump back up to root directory, the one with the WORKSPACE file inside of it. Let's list the contents within:

```
chapter_03$ ls
WORKSPACE
src (or your favorite directory name)
```

Additionally, let's confirm the contents within the src directory. This

```
chapter_03$ ls src
BUILD    HelloWorld.java
```

This is the clean state of your Bazel project, where nothing has been built. Let's change that.

Build the Binary

To build your first project, run the following from the command line:

```
chapter_03$ bazel build src:HelloWorld
```

Breaking the arguments to the bazel command down a bit

- build

  - This specifies that you are building/compiling/assembling the given target.

- src

  - This specifies the directory which contains your desired build target.

  - In this example, the directory is rather shallow; however, you can (and will) specify any number of valid directory paths to supplement this argument.

- :HelloWorld

  - This is the actual build target within the src directory.

  - A given directory can have one or more buildable targets in Bazel.

Assuming that all has gone to plan, your output should be something like this:

```
INFO: Analysed target //src:HelloWorld (19 packages loaded, 550 targets
     configured).
INFO: Found 1 target...
Target //src:HelloWorld up-to-date:
 bazel-bin/src/HelloWorld.jar
 bazel-bin/src/HelloWorld
INFO: Elapsed time: 0.144s, Critical Path: 0.00s
INFO: 0 processes.
INFO: Build completed successfully, 1 total action.
```

Running the Binary

Having built your executable, you can run it using the following:

```
chapter_03$ bazel-bin/src/HelloWorld
Hello, World!
```

However, for practical development, you will not want to constantly flip between building the executable and then directly executing the binary. Fortunately, you don't have to; Bazel provides the facility to directly build and run your executable.

Similar to how you built the executable in the first place, you can directly run the executable via

```
chapter_03% bazel run src:HelloWorld

INFO: Analysed target //src:HelloWorld (0 packages loaded, 0 targets
      configured).
INFO: Found 1 target...
Target //src:HelloWorld up-to-date:
  bazel-bin/src/HelloWorld.jar
  bazel-bin/src/HelloWorld
INFO: Elapsed time: 0.217s, Critical Path: 0.07s
INFO: 1 process: 1 worker.
INFO: Build completed successfully, 2 total actions
INFO: Build completed successfully, 2 total actions
Hello, World!
```

Note   One item to notice in both runs is the line regarding (*X* packages loaded, *Y* targets configured). This provides a rough indication about the state of the cache for your project. In the first example, these were nonzero values, indicating that work needed to be done on dependencies in order to produce your target. In the second example, both of these were 0, indicating that the build should be fully cached. Bazel loads packages and targets only when something changes, intelligently rebuilding only what is necessary.

Creating and Using Dependencies

Creating a single binary is fine; however, it is certainly not practical for development. In practice, we want to separate our programs into finer grain components. Finer grain components have many advantages, including being more shareable, easier to test, faster to build, and easier to optimize the build.

In this particular case, there isn't much we can pull out of our original example, so let's add some new functionality.

Within your src directory, create a new file IntMultiplier.java and add the following code.

Listing 3-3. IntMultiplier.java

```java
public class IntMultiplier {
  private int a;
  private int b;

  public IntMultiplier(int a, int b) {
    this.a = a;
    this.b = b;
  }

  public int GetProduct() {
    return a * b;
  }
}
```

Don't add anything to the BUILD file yet; we will first attempt to add our new class to our binary.

Listing 3-4. Adding IntMultiplier to HelloWorld.java

```java
public class HelloWorld {
  public static void main(String[] args) {
    System.out.println("Hello, World!");
    IntMultiplier im = new IntMultiplier(3, 4);
    System.out.println(im.GetProduct());
  }
}
```

Now let's try to run our build for HelloWorld again:

```
chapter_03% bazel run src:HelloWorld

INFO: Analysed target //src:HelloWorld (0 packages loaded, 0 targets
      configured).
INFO: Found 1 target...
ERROR: /Users/pj/Dropbox/Books/Beginning_Bazel/code_samples/chapter_03/src/
      BUILD:6:1: Building src/HelloWorld.jar (1 source file) failed (Exit 1)
src/HelloWorld.java:5: error: cannot find symbol
        IntMultiplier im = new IntMultiplier(3, 4);
        ^
  symbol:   class IntMultiplier
  location: class HelloWorld
src/HelloWorld.java:5: error: cannot find symbol
        IntMultiplier im = new IntMultiplier(3, 4);
                               ^
  symbol:   class IntMultiplier
  location: class HelloWorld
Target //src:HelloWorld failed to build
Use --verbose_failures to see the command lines of failed build steps.
INFO: Elapsed time: 0.246s, Critical Path: 0.10s
INFO: 0 processes.
FAILED: Build did NOT complete successfully
```

In this case, the build failed because it was unable to find IntMultiplier. This illustrates one of Bazel's most important qualities: there is nothing implicit in the build; you need to explicitly specify everything, including all dependencies. Bazel will not automagically find anything in the same directory, package, and so on.

We can solve this issue in one of two ways:

- Add the new source files to the binary.

- Create a new library upon which the binary will depend.

We will explore both of these methods.

Adding IntMulitplier.java to java_binary

In this case, we can just add IntMultiplier.java as another source for the HelloWorld build target.

Listing 3-5. Adding to the HelloWorld srcs

```
java_binary(
    name = "HelloWorld",
    srcs = [
        "HelloWorld.java",
        "IntMultiplier.java",
    ],
)
```

Now, let's try rerunning HelloWorld:

```
chapter_03% bazel run src:HelloWorld
INFO: Analysed target //src:HelloWorld (0 packages loaded, 0 targets
      configured).
INFO: Found 1 target...
Target //src:HelloWorld up-to-date:
  bazel-bin/src/HelloWorld.jar
  bazel-bin/src/HelloWorld
INFO: Elapsed time: 0.141s, Critical Path: 0.00s
INFO: 0 processes.
INFO: Build completed successfully, 1 total action
INFO: Build completed successfully, 1 total action
Hello, World!
12
```

By explicitly listing the files the target depends upon, HelloWorld is able to successfully build and run.

However, while this solution works, it is still sub-optimal; as it stands, IntMultiplier could easily be reused in other places; at the moment, it is locked within the HelloWorld binary.

Creating a java_library Dependency

Instead of adding the file to the HelloWorld build target, let's instead create an entirely separate dependency. This time, instead of creating a java_binary build target, we are going to introduce a new type of build target, java_library.

As the name implies, the java_library build target is meant to encapsulate some shared collection of Java functionality. Once created, the java_library may then be depended upon by other build targets (which includes other java_library build targets).

Listing 3-6. Creating the java_library dependency

```
java_library(
      name = "LibraryExample",
      srcs = ["IntMultiplier.java"],
)
```

Having created a new build target, let's build it directly:

```
chapter_03% bazel build src:LibraryExample
INFO: Analysed target //src:LibraryExample (1 packages loaded, 2 targets
      configured).
INFO: Found 1 target...
Target //src:LibraryExample up-to-date:
  bazel-bin/src/libLibraryExample.jar
INFO: Elapsed time: 0.203s, Critical Path: 0.06s
INFO: 1 process: 1 worker.
INFO: Build completed successfully, 2 total actions
```

However, as expected and in contrast to our HelloWorld example, we are not able to run this particular build target. Attempting to do so results in the following error:

```
chapter_03% bazel run src:LibraryExample
ERROR: Cannot run target //src:LibraryExample: Not executable
INFO: Elapsed time: 0.097s
INFO: 0 processes.
FAILED: Build did NOT complete successfully (0 packages loaded)
FAILED: Build did NOT complete successfully (0 packages loaded)
```

Depending on Build Targets

Now that we have created the build target, we will make HelloWorld depend upon the target.

Listing 3-7. Adding a dependency to HelloWorld

```
java_binary(
      name = "HelloWorld",
      srcs = [ "HelloWorld.java"],
      deps = [":LibraryExample"],
)
```

Now let's rerun HelloWorld:

```
chapter_03% bazel run src:HelloWorld
INFO: Analysed target //src:HelloWorld (1 packages loaded, 4 targets
      configured).
INFO: Found 1 target...
Target //src:HelloWorld up-to-date:
  bazel-bin/src/HelloWorld.jar
  bazel-bin/src/HelloWorld
INFO: Elapsed time: 0.955s, Critical Path: 0.78s
INFO: 3 processes: 1 darwin-sandbox, 2 worker.
INFO: Build completed successfully, 7 total actions
INFO: Build completed successfully, 7 total actions
Hello, World!
12
```

The pattern of binary and library targets in Bazel is a universal pair of constructs, regardless of language. Generally speaking, the number of <insert language>_binary targets you create will be relatively small; they will correspond to the number of output executables you wish to create. In contrast, the number of <insert language>_library build targets you create will be relatively large.

Testing Your Build Targets

One of the chief advantages of creating smaller build units is that they become far easier to test. Having created some modular functionality, let's set up a test to verify the functionality.

Setting Up Testing Dependencies

Prior to creating a test, we will first need to set up some required dependencies.

Within your project's root directory, create a new directory, third_party, and two sub-directories therein, hamcrest and junit:

```
chapter_03$ mkdir third_party
chapter_03$ mkdir third_party/hamcrest
chapter_03$ mkdir third_party/junit
```

Follow the instructions from the following site https://github.com/junit-team/junit4/wiki/download-and-install to download the following jars:

- hamcrest-core-1.3.jar

- junit-4.12.jar

Move the jars into their respective directories under third_party. In order to utilize these jars, we will make use of yet another type of build target, java_import.

Let's create a new BUILD file to contain the java_import build target.

Listing 3-8. BUILD file for third_party targets

```
package(default_visibility = ["//visibility:public"])

java_import(
        name = "junit4",
        jars = [
                "hamcrest/hamcrest-core-1.3.jar",
                "junit/junit-4.12.jar",
        ]
)
```

Note   A sharp observer will note that we have slipped in a new directive, package, into the BUILD file. We will dive further into this in a later chapter to control the visibility of build targets toward other targets. For now, it is sufficient to know that this directive enables the targets contained within this BUILD file to be visible to any other BUILD targets in any other BUILD file.

Save the BUILD file to the third_party directory. You can test that it is set up correctly by running

```
chapter_03$ bazel build third_party:junit4
INFO: Analysed target //third_party:junit4 (2 packages loaded, 25 targets
     configured).
INFO: Found 1 target...
Target //third_party:junit4 up-to-date (nothing to build)
INFO: Elapsed time: 0.157s, Critical Path: 0.00s
INFO: 0 processes.
INFO: Build completed successfully, 1 total action
```

Creating the java_test Build Target

Now let's create a test for our functionality using the java_test build target.

Listing 3-9. IntMultiplierTest.java

```
import static org.junit.Assert.assertEquals;

import org.junit.Test;

public class IntMultiplierTest {
        @Test
        public void testIntMultiplier() throws Exception {
          IntMultiplier im = new IntMultiplier(3, 4);
          assertEquals(12, im.GetProduct());
        }
}
```

Save to src/IntMultiplierTest.java.

Now let's add a new build target to the BUILD file.

Listing 3-10. Adding java_test to BUILD

```
java_test(
        name = "LibraryExampleTest",
        srcs = ["IntMultiplierTest.java"],
        deps = [
                ":LibraryExample",
                "//third_party:junit4",
        ],
        test_class = "IntMultiplierTest",
)
```

Run your newly created test:

```
chapter_03$ bazel test src:LibraryExampleTest
INFO: Build options --collect_code_coverage, --instrumentation_filter, and
        --test_timeout have changed, discarding analysis cache.
INFO: Analysed target //src:LibraryExampleTest (0 packages loaded,
        617 targets configured).
INFO: Found 1 test target...
Target //src:LibraryExampleTest up-to-date:
  bazel-bin/src/LibraryExampleTest.jar
  bazel-bin/src/LibraryExampleTest
INFO: Elapsed time: 2.710s, Critical Path: 2.40s
INFO: 3 processes: 1 darwin-sandbox, 2 worker.
INFO: Build completed successfully, 7 total actions
//src:LibraryExampleTest
PASSED in 0.4s

Executed 1 out of 1 test: 1 test passes.
INFO: Build completed successfully, 7 total actions
```

As expected, the test passes.

Just to verify, let's add one more test case. This time, let's initially create a failing test, just to see what happens.

Listing 3-11. Add a failing test

```
public class IntMultiplierTest {
      @Test
      public void testIntMultiplier() throws Exception {
        IntMultiplier im = new IntMultiplier(3, 4);
        assertEquals(12, im.GetProduct());
      }

      @Test
      public void testIntMultiplier_Failure() throws Exception {
        IntMultiplier im = new IntMultiplier(4, 5);
        assertEquals(21, im.GetProduct());
      }
}
```

Save the file and re-execute the test:

```
chapter_03$ bazel test src:LibraryExampleTest
INFO: Analysed target //src:LibraryExampleTest (20 packages loaded,
      617 targets configured).
INFO: Found 1 test target...
FAIL: //src:LibraryExampleTest (see <some_local_directory>/execroot/__
      main__/bazel-out/darwin-fastbuild/testlogs/src/LibraryExampleTest/
      test.log)
Target //src:LibraryExampleTest up-to-date:
  bazel-bin/src/LibraryExampleTest.jar
  bazel-bin/src/LibraryExampleTest
INFO: Elapsed time: 13.038s, Critical Path: 2.91s
INFO: 3 processes: 1 darwin-sandbox, 2 worker.
INFO: Build completed, 1 test FAILED, 7 total actions
//src:LibraryExampleTest
FAILED in 0.3s
```

<some_local_directory>/execroot/__main__/bazel-out/darwin-fastbuild/
testlogs/src/LibraryExampleTest/test.log

From the (rather obvious) failure, Bazel outputs info to the aforementioned test.log
file. Cracking open this file reveals the following.

Listing 3-12.   Failure found in test.log file

```
There was 1 failure:
1) testIntMultiplier_Failure(IntMultiplierTest)
java.lang.AssertionError: expected:<21> but was:<20>
```

Note that the actual output may be vastly more verbose, but the preceding code is sufficient for us to diagnose and repair the problem. Let's correct the issue and rerun the test.

Listing 3-13.   Correcting the failing test

```
public class IntMultiplierTest {
        ...

        @Test
        public void testIntMultiplier_Failure() throws Exception {
          IntMultiplier im = new IntMultiplier(4, 5);
          assertEquals(20, im.GetProduct());
        }
}
```

Rerunning the test:

```
chapter_03$ bazel test src:LibraryExampleTest
INFO: Analysed target //src:LibraryExampleTest (0 packages loaded,
     0 targets configured).
INFO: Found 1 test target...
Target //src:LibraryExampleTest up-to-date:
  bazel-bin/src/LibraryExampleTest.jar
  bazel-bin/src/LibraryExampleTest
INFO: Elapsed time: 0.717s, Critical Path: 0.56s
INFO: 2 processes: 1 darwin-sandbox, 1 worker.
INFO: Build completed successfully, 3 total actions
//src:LibraryExampleTest
PASSED in 0.3s
```

Build (and Clean) the World

Before we wrap up, let's look at a couple more pieces of core Bazel functionality.

Build Everything (In a Directory)

In the preceding examples, we built each of the build targets individually. While this is fine when doing development on individual components, this is obviously not a scalable process.

Bazel has built-in functionality for building multiple types of targets at the same time. For example, instead of building each of the build targets within the src directory, we could order Bazel to build all of them at once by running

```
chapter_03$ bazel build src:all
INFO: Analysed 3 targets (20 packages loaded, 619 targets configured).
INFO: Found 3 targets...
INFO: Elapsed time: 8.892s, Critical Path: 5.87s
INFO: 9 processes: 6 darwin-sandbox, 3 worker.
INFO: Build completed successfully, 16 total actions
```

In this case, :all is not a particular build target; it is a meta-target that tells Bazel to literally build all build targets within a given package (i.e., directory).

In a similar fashion, we could tell Bazel to build everything in the third_party directory as well:

```
chapter_03$ bazel build third_party:all
INFO: Analysed target //third_party:junit4 (13 packages loaded, 520 targets
    configured).
INFO: Found 1 target...
Target //third_party:junit4 up-to-date (nothing to build)
INFO: Elapsed time: 1.467s, Critical Path: 0.00s
INFO: 0 processes.
INFO: Build completed successfully, 1 total action
```

The :all target works not only for building but for all of the Bazel commands (e.g., bazel test <insert target>).

It might already be obvious, but do not name any of your build targets "all." This will only lead to confusion.

Build Everything (At This Directory and Below)

Once again, the preceding build all command works great when dealing with particular directories; however, it would again become tedious if having to build for all directories in this manner. Fortunately, Bazel once again comes to our rescue with yet another command to help out.

Run the following command from your workspace root:

```
chapter_03$ bazel build ...
INFO: Analysed 4 targets (20 packages loaded, 620 targets configured).
INFO: Found 4 targets...
INFO: Elapsed time: 7.234s, Critical Path: 5.78s
INFO: 9 processes: 6 darwin-sandbox, 3 worker.
INFO: Build completed successfully, 16 total actions
```

This time, the "..." meta-target is telling Bazel to build everything at the current directory as well as everything below this directory. When executed at the root level of your workspace, this will build *everything* in your workspace. Use caution when building like this, although this may very well be a great way to start your morning after updating your local repository.

As with the :all meta-target, the "..." meta-target will also work with the other Bazel commands (e.g., test).

Additionally, you can scope "..." to particular directories. For instance, you could have used "bazel build src/..." in order to build everything under the src directory.

Clean (Mostly) Everything

As good as Bazel is at managing dependencies, you may get to some point in time where you need to just clean the world and start over. Cleaning in Bazel is as simple as

```
chapter_03$ bazel clean
INFO: Starting clean.
```

That's really it. If you do a quick `ls` on your root directory, you will notice that none of the `bazel-*` directories are there any longer; all of the outputs, caches, and so on have been removed. Of course, they will return upon your next Bazel command that builds your targets.

Final Word

Congratulations! You have just created and wired together your first set of Bazel targets, encompassing a host of different pieces of functionality:

- `java_binary`
    - Representing and creating a Java executable
- `java_library`
    - Encapsulating a shareable piece of Java functionality
- `java_import`
    - Wrapping one or more preexisting jar files into a unit that can be depended upon
- `java_test`
    - Creating a test for verifying the expected behavior of the `java_library`

With even this small subset of Bazel build targets, you have sufficient functionality to create, organize, test, and run a Java program.

Notably, this chapter focused exclusively on Java targets in order to illustrate Bazel functionality. However, the pattern of {language}_binary, {language}_library, and {language}_test will become familiar for the various languages that Bazel (and its extensions) supports.

For example:

- C/C++ (built-in support from Bazel)
    - `cc_binary`, `cc_library`, `cc_test`

- Python (built-in support from Bazel)

    - `py_binary`, `py_library`, `py_test`

- Go (supplied by external rules)

    - `go_binary`, `go_library`, `go_test`

Of course, each language supported by Bazel may also have some language-specific constructs (e.g., `java_import`); however, even in these cases, there are features that are largely common to all types of build targets (e.g., name, visibility, dependencies, etc.).

In the following chapters, we will focus less on a specific language and dive further into some of the structural elements of Bazel itself, namely, around the `BUILD` and the `WORKSPACE` files.

EXERCISE – PYTHON HELLOWORLD

Throughout this chapter, we have only been focused on creating Java targets. However, out of the box, Bazel has the ability to target Java, Python, and C++. Now that you have done the HelloWorld exercise for Java, create it using Python.

Since one of the hallmarks of Bazel is handling multiple languages at the same time, you can create a similar set of `HelloWorld` Python targets within the same BUILD file as your Java targets. Practically speaking, you are unlikely to do this in real life; however, it does illustrate Bazel's ability to handle multiple targets, across languages, within the same BUILD file. Your Python executable will end up in a py_binary build target.

Finally, you can also create similar `IntMultiplier` functionality in its own `py_library` build target as well as a corresponding set of tests within its `py_test` build target. Unlike Java, Python comes "batteries included" and packages up its own unit test framework, obviating the need to create something similar to the `junit4` build target for Java.

CHAPTER 4

WORKSPACE File Functionality

In our last chapter, we created and ran our first Bazel project, focusing mostly on the bare minimum to get something up and running. During the course of that chapter, we employed two specially named files: BUILD and, to a much lesser extent, WORKSPACE. While the use of the BUILD file was apparent, we (intentionally) left the WORKSPACE file alone. In this chapter, we are going to explore a greater set of functionalities for the WORKSPACE file.

Note This chapter will give a high-level overview of the WORKSPACE file; however, performing the exercises will be crucial to starting to get a feel for how it actually works.

WORKSPACE Files

In the last chapter, we left the WORKSPACE file completely blank. For that particular example, we did not need to add anything else, since we were only making use of all the functionality that comes out of the box from Bazel.

In particular, there were two distinct characteristics of that last exercise:

- All code was within a single, local repository.

- The only rules and build targets required came out of the box from Bazel.

In practice, however, this combination is usually not viable for most projects. You *will* need to depend upon additional functionality and, in all likelihood, employ other languages or types of build targets for your projects. The WORKSPACE file is the place to set the stage for the body of functionality and rules required by your project.

© P.J. McNerney 2020
P.J. McNerney, *Beginning Bazel*, https://doi.org/10.1007/978-1-4842-5194-2_4

Adding New Rules to WORKSPACE

As stated earlier, Bazel comes with out-of-the-box support for a number of build Rules. For example, there are rules that define how to build, compile, link, etc. for C++, Java, Python, and so on. Additionally, a vanilla Bazel project also defines utility rules that are used to define how resources (e.g., data files) should be packaged and referenced within your project.

One of the most powerful aspects of Bazel is the ability to add new rules to expand its capabilities. By adding new rules to our project's workspace, we can add in retrieve remote dependencies, add in new languages, and more.

Notably, there are rules which are packaged with Bazel that are not automatically loaded by default. This enables you as a project creator to have explicit control over what rules you want to have available within your project.

The basic command that we will use to load in new rules is load, which is built into Bazel.

Note   The load command will be used both within WORKSPACE and BUILD files. As you might have guessed, we will end up using this to explicitly pull into new types of functionality into our BUILD file as well.

The basic structure for using load is

```
load("//local/path/to/my:file.bzl", "symbol_to_load")
```

This will cause load to pull in the file found within the local path and load the specified symbol into the local environment; when placed into the WORKSPACE file, this will load the symbol into the local environment.

For a practical example of using load, we will used it to pull the http_archive rule into the WORKSPACE. Let's create a new project directory. This time, however, we will cheat a bit and copy our last chapter's work. Before we copy, we will first need to clean out any existing build outputs, to avoid accidentally pulling them over:

```
$ cd chapter_03
chapter_03$ bazel clean
chapter_03$ cd ..
$ cp -r chapter_03 chapter_04
$ cd chapter_04
```

In the previous chapter, we had left the WORKSPACE file completely empty and relied solely on the build-in rules. Now let's start to add a bit of new functionality into the WORKSPACE file.

In your favorite editor, open the WORKSPACE file and write the following.

Listing 4-1. A simple load command

```
load("@bazel_tools//tools/build_defs/repo:http.bzl", "http_archive")
```

Save that file to disk.

Congratulations! You've just added some functionality into your WORKSPACE file. Of course, that functionality does not actually do anything at the moment (we will get to that in the next section).

Note   A sharp observer will once again notice the introduction of a new file type: .bzl. Although outside the scope of this book, it is sufficient to know that .bzl files are used to define rules for Bazel (e.g., build rules) and give us the abillty to expand Bazel's capabilities (e.g., the addition of new languages).

A Deeper Dive into the Load Path

If you are taking a close look at the load path from the preceding example, you might notice something interesting: that particular path does not exist within your file system. So, where is this coming from?

The very first element of the path is @bazel_tools. The @ signifies to Bazel that you are loading from a particular Bazel repository, called bazel_tools. The file path beneath to the right of bazel_tools specifies a particular path to a file *within that repository*.

This is an important detail, since this is going to become very important shortly. As your project begins to reference functionality found in other Bazel repositories, you will disambiguate those repositories using a name. This allows you to create absolute paths to the build targets you require for your project.

At this point in time, you still haven't pulled in any external repositories, so where did bazel_tools actually come from? The bazel_tools repository is special and (sort of) comes "out of the box."

This is essential since it comes with some important functionality, not the least of which is the ability to pull in other repositories. Consider this a bootstrapping repository you acquire by virtue of installing Bazel and creating a WORKSPACE.

Finding the bazel_tools Repository

If you decide to go hunting a bit, you can find the location of the bazel_tools repository in a project. First, however, let's clean up our existing project:

```
chapter_04$ bazel clean
```

Now, if you attempt to locate the bazel_tools repository in our current project, you will be left wanting:

```
chapter_04$ ls -1
WORKSPACE
src
third_party
```

Notice that all we have here are the directories and files that we had created previously; our clean command has eradicated all build products, dependencies, outputs, and so on. At this point in time, the Bazel project is effectively untouched; no Bazel commands have actually been executed. Bazel strives to never download more than it needs at a given point in time; as such it won't even download bazel_tools to a given WORKSPACE unless it absolutely needs to.

Now, let's rerun a valid build command from the prior chapter:

```
chapter_04$ bazel build src:LibraryExampleTest
chapter_04$ ls -1
WORKSPACE
bazel-bin
bazel-chapter_04
bazel-out
bazel-testlogs
src
third_party
```

This time, we're going to dive a bit deeper into the generated files, specifically into bazel-chapter_04:

```
chapter_04$ cd bazel-chapter_04
chapter_04/bazel-chapter_04$ ls -1
bazel-out
external
src
third_party

chapter_04$ cd external
chapter_04/bazel-chapter_04/external$ ls -1
bazel_tools
(other directories may be here)
```

Congratulations! You've found the repository. Notably, where it is located illustrates a few important points about Bazel.

Note   For the curious, if you continue to explore through the bazel_tools directory, you will find the tools/build_defs/repo dIrectory there. This is where you previously had loaded the http.bzl file from.

First, that your project is individually meant to be the definitive source of truth. There is not a central location across all of your projects where a common bazel_tools repository exists; each project is meant to get its own version of a repository (although this doesn't prevent Bazel from doing some optimization behind the scenes to share repositories via file linking).

Secondly, that Bazel will not download a dependency unless it is *absolutely required* to do so. We will revisit this later on in this chapter; however, even if you create new external dependencies in your WORKSPACE file, if you never use anything from said dependencies, *Bazel will not download them.* This goes to the heart of the notion that by making everything explicit, Bazel can do some cool optimizations.

Loading Multiple Rules at the Same Time

Before we leave this section, it is worthwhile to know that it is possible to have multiple rules within the same file. While you could execute multiple *load* commands in order to pull in the desired functionality, you can also just retrieve all the necessary symbols at once.

The format for this is

```
load("//local/path/to/my:file.bzl", "symbol_to_load_1", "symbol_to_load_2",
"symbol_to_load_3")
```

That is, you can simply append to the load command as many symbols that you want to load from a given file. For a practical example, refer to the following.

Listing 4-2. A load command that pulls in multiple symbols

```
load("@bazel_tools//tools/build_defs/repo:http.bzl", "http_archive",
"http_file")
```

This will load both the *http_archive* and *http_file* symbols into your workspace.

Referencing Other Dependencies

In the last chapter, we explicitly downloaded the JUnit libraries and added these directly to our project. This fits really well into the model that Bazel prefers (i.e., a monorepo).

However, Bazel provides the ability to reference other external dependencies in a couple of different ways. This provides some additional flexibility by allowing you to add to your project without ingesting the dependencies explicitly.

There are a few rules in the WORKSPACE file which can be used to pull down dependencies external to your project. In practice, two of the most prominent ones (which you will see in various Bazel projects) are

- http_archive
- git_repository

Note that while these rules used to be out of the box for earlier versions of Bazel, you need to load them explicitly to get them into your project.

Each of these rules are designed to retrieve remote Bazel repositories and make their contains targets available as dependencies for your project.

http_archive

http_archive is used to reference and retrieve a compressed Bazel repository, given a path to said compressed file. Once the compressed repository has been retrieved, it is decompressed, and the contained rules, targets, and so on can be used within your project.

The most basic, stripped-down form of http_archive is the following.

Listing 4-3. Example http_archive

```
http_archive (
        name = "foo",
        urls = ["http://my_favorite_url.com/path/to/archive.zip"],
)
```

Let's break down the preceding code a little bit. The preceding rule specifies to retrieve the repository from the location *http://my_favorite_url.com/path/to/archive.zip*. Assuming this is successful, the archived file will be retrieved, downloaded, and decompressed (if it hasn't been already), making the content available for use.

Now, earlier we discussed how we needed to use the label bazel_tools in order to use any functionality within that repository. In a similar fashion, in order to make use of any functionality in our new repository foo, we need to use label @foo.

To make all of this a little more concrete, let's get a real http_archive example. Let's add the following to your chapter_04 WORKSPACE file.

Listing 4-4. http_archive for Go language rules

```
load("@bazel_tools//tools/build_defs/repo:http.bzl", "http_archive")
http_archive (
        name = "io_bazel_rules_go",
        urls = ["https://github.com/bazelbuild/rules_go/releases/download/
                v0.19.5/rules_go-v0.19.5.tar.gz"],
)
```

Save your WORKSPACE file.

As you can imagine, this will pull down the compressed repository for the Go language rules and decompress it, making the repository's targets available for use. As we explored earlier, this repository will ultimately end up in the chapter_04/bazel-chapter_04/external directory (notably, it won't be there right away, for reasons we discussed earlier in the chapter).

In order to make use of any functionality within the repository, we need to make sure we are properly specifying said functionality. To illustrate, let's add the following to the WORKSPACE file, just under our http_archive directive.

Listing 4-5. Retrieving functionality for Go

```
load("@io_bazel_rules_go//go:deps.bzl", "go_rules_dependencies",
"go_register_toolchains")
```

Save this to your WORKSPACE file.

You should notice that you needed to specify @io_bazel_rules_go to form the correct path to get access to the underlying functionality.

git_repository

While http_archive is focused on retrieving a compressed archive of a Bazel repository (whether it is part of an SCM system or not), git_repository is used to clone a git repository and check it out at a given commit (or tag).

Once again, let's start with a bare-bones example. Note that we need to explicitly load the git_repository rule as we did with http_archive.

Listing 4-6. Loading and using the git_repository

```
load("@bazel_tools//tools/build_defs/repo:git.bzl", "git_repository")
git_repository(
    name = "foo",
    remote = "http://my_favorite_url.com/path/to/repo.git",
    commit = "some_commit_hash_to_check_out_repo",
)
```

Having broken down http_archive, there are some features that look very similar. In this case, name operates identically, acting as a disambiguating label for the repository. Similar to http_archive's urls parameter, remote specifies the path to the Git repo that we want to clone (e.g., on some place like GitHub.com). The only major difference is the commit, in order to specify the version of the repo to actually retrieve.

Retrieving a Git Repository

Once again, now let's motivate this with a real example. Add the following to your WORKSPACE file.

Listing 4-7. Retrieving the repository for Go

```
load("@bazel_tools//tools/build_defs/repo:git.bzl", "git_repository")
git_repository(
    name = "io_bazel_rules_go",
    remote = "https://github.com/bazelbuild/rules_go.git",
    commit = "f5cfc31d4e8de28bf19d0fb1da2ab8f4be0d2cde",
)
```

Caution   The specific commit hash used here is only current as of the time of this writing; you may need to check the repo for a more current one.

Prior to saving this into your WORKSPACE file, it is highly recommended to comment out the http_archive version of the same request. Otherwise, you will have the same name represented between your http_archive version and your git_repository version. Bazel will disambiguate which one "wins" by taking the last one in the file; however, for the sake of clarity, you shouldn't add ambiguity to your WORKSPACE file in your dependencies.

Save your WORKSPACE file.

Fine Print on git_repository

Although git_repository clones a remote git repository into your Bazel project, this does not actually confer the ability to work with it as you would with a normal git repository. That is, you cannot go into the directory that contains the Git repo (e.g., bazel-chapter_04/external/<name of git repository>) and start performing a typical set of git operations (e.g., commit, push, etc.). And, given where the repository is placed, this should make sense: all of the bazel-* directories are ephemeral. All of them can be removed by a simple act of bazel clean, which could easily eliminate any locally created changes.

One way to make edits to an external git repository and have it reflect into your project is to clone that repo separately, make and commit your changes, and *then* update your project's commit hash to match with the newly created commits. Admittedly, this may not be the smoothest workflow; however, remember that Bazel constantly is focused on reproducibility. Explicitly tracking the dependencies is one of the keys that gives Bazel its power.

There is another way to work with `git_repository;` instead of using the commit hash, we refer to a tag added for the commit. An example can be seen as follows.

Listing 4-8. Using the tag instead of the commit hash

```
git_repository(
    name = "foo",
    remote = "http://my_favorite_url.com/path/to/repo.git",
    tag = "<my_favorite_tag>"
)
```

Now instead of being locked onto a specific commit hash, you track to a particular tag; if you make updates to the Git repo (and subsequently update the tag), your project will get the version corresponding to the tag.

As an alternative to both tag and commit, you can also use "branch" to refer to a specific branch of a Git repo.

Note   You must choose among "tag," "commit," or "branch" to refer to a particular version of the code; you cannot use more than one at the same time.

While this makes working with external repos more convenient, this provides a **much** weaker guarantee than the commit hash. While this can be convenient for doing development, it can also lead to issues in practice, since you are dependent upon what amounts to a floating version of code.

http_archive vs. git_repository

Both `http_archive` and `git_repository` are tools for referencing external Bazel repositories; however, this raises the question "Given the option between the two, which should I use?" For example, GitHub provides both git repositories (obviously) and archives.

As a default, the recommendation from Bazel is to prefer `http_archive`. This makes sense, since it provides the strongest guarantee of reproducibility (i.e., the archive is static for a given version). It is also faster to download and extract an archive than to clone a reposition. Additionally, it obviates the need to install git to build a project. This is especially a good idea for dependencies whose versions are expected to change slowly.

Note   Strictly speaking, the contents of even an http_archive URL *may* change. In order to strengthen the guarantee for retrieving the correct files for the sake of reproducibility, there is *another* attribute, sha256, which contains the expected SHA-256 of the archive to retrieve. Although this field is omitted for simplicity here, for real development, you should set this field in order to ensure the hermeticity of the build.

On the other hand, if an archive is unavailable or you *need* to work with external dependencies that are changing rapidly, then `git_repository` may make a lot more sense (especially given the aforementioned ability to work with git tags).

As a last word, Bazel projects favor being monolithic, so one avenue to consider is to *avoid* using external dependencies and pull in the necessary code into your project. This is not always possible or convenient but *does* provide the strongest guarantees for your builds.

Employing a New Language

While Bazel comes with several languages out of the box, we need to be able to add more languages as needed to our project. In case you have not guessed it, we will add support for Go into our project.

Let's make use of some of the tools that we have picked up along the way. Make sure the following is within your WORKSPACE file.

Listing 4-9. Loading the Go language rules

```
load("@bazel_tools//tools/build_defs/repo:http.bzl", "http_archive")
http_archive (
        name = "io_bazel_rules_go",
        urls = ["https://github.com/bazelbuild/rules_go/releases/download/
            v0.19.5/rules_go-v0.19.5.tar.gz"],
```

```
)
load("@io_bazel_rules_go//go:deps.bzl", "go_rules_dependencies",
"go_register_toolchains")
go_rules_dependencies()
go_register_toolchains()
```

Save the WORKSPACE file.

You've seen most of that example previously, with the exception of the last two lines. The last two lines invoke the loaded rules to set up the Go language with your project.

Note   Unlike many constructs and patterns in Bazel, the above two lines should not be considered a canonical example for all languages. Each new language has its own set of one or more rules for setup, so the function names will likely be slightly different each time.

Having set up the Go rules, let's create a new target with them. Once again, we'll start with a basic example.

```
chapter_04$ cd src
chapter_04/src$ touch hello_world.go
```

Let's create a simple Go program.

Listing 4-10. Hello World in Go

```
package main

import "fmt"

func main() {
        fmt.Println("Hello, World!")
}
```

Save this to hello_world.go.

Now, let's crack open the BUILD file in the src directory so we can create the Go target. However, prior to actually creating the target, we need to explicitly load up the Go rules.

Add the following to the BUILD file.

Listing 4-11. Loading the Go language rules

```
load("@io_bazel_rules_go//go:def.bzl", "go_binary")
```

Note that we are loading up using the label @io_bazel_rules_go in order to correctly refer to the packages we need for the rules. Before we save, let's also add the new Go target.

Listing 4-12. Create the go_binary target

```
go_binary(
        name = "hello_world_go",
        srcs = ["hello_world.go"],
)
```

Save to the BUILD file. Now we should be able to actually build and run the target:

```
chapter_04/src$ bazel run :hello_world_go
INFO: Analysed target //src:go_hello_world (23 packages loaded, 6239
     targets configured).
INFO: Found 1 target...
Target //src:go_hello_world up-to-date:
  bazel-bin/src/darwin_amd64_stripped/go_hello_world
INFO: Elapsed time: 3.221s, Critical Path: 1.08s
INFO: 6 processes: 6 darwin-sandbox.
INFO: Build completed successfully, 10 total actions
INFO: Build completed successfully, 10 total actions
Hello, World!
```

Congratulations! You now have added a new language and created a target for it!

Locating the Go Language Rules Repository

Earlier we looked for the `bazel_tools` repository, which only appeared after we had performed a build that actually required it. In the same fashion, you should now have a repository for the Go language rules. Let's take a quick look to confirm:

```
chapter_04/src$ cd ../bazel-chapter_04/external
chapter_04/bazel-chapter_04/external$ ls -1
bazel_tools
io_bazel_rules_go
(possible other repos)
```

Previously, Bazel only pulls down the dependencies required to build your requested target. If you performed a *clean* action, followed by a build of a non-Go target (e.g., the earlier Java targets), you would find that `io_bazel_rules_go` would **not** exist within your `bazel-chapter_04/external` directory, despite the fact that both targets exist in the same BUILD file.

EXERCISE – ADD YET ANOTHER LANGUAGE

Throughout the section on the WORKSPACE file, we've been building up the knowledge for adding a new language into your project. Now that you have the tools for this, you should continue to explore adding new languages to your project.

Go to `https://github.com/bazelbuild` and look through the various rules packages they have available. Notably, while there will be many common languages there, some rule sets might be outside of the bazelbuild organization. If you don't find a language to your liking, you can find an even larger list at Awesome Bazel (`https://awesomebazel.com`). Select your favorite language, set up your WORKSPACE file, and create a build target for that language.

CHAPTER 5

A Simple Echo Client/ Server Program

In the last chapter, you learned the basics of the WORKSPACE file, learning how to add external dependencies, including new languages. In this chapter, we are going to build off of that work to create a simple pair of programs, in different languages (one in Java, the other in Go), to round trip messages between the two of them.

Setting Up Your Workspace

Let's create a new directory for our work:

```
$ mkdir chapter_05
$ cd chapter_05
chapter_05$ touch WORKSPACE
```

We are going to pull in the Go rules that we utilized in the last chapter. Open your newly created WORKSPACE file and add the following.

Listing 5-1. Adding in the Go rules

```
load("@bazel_tools//tools/build_defs/repo:http.bzl", "http_archive")
http_archive (
        name = "io_bazel_rules_go",
        urls = ["https://github.com/bazelbuild/rules_go/releases/download/
                v0.19.5/rules_go-v0.19.5.tar.gz"],
)
```

© P.J. McNerney 2020
P.J. McNerney, *Beginning Bazel*, https://doi.org/10.1007/978-1-4842-5194-2_5

```
load("@io_bazel_rules_go/go:deps.bzl", "go_rules_dependencies",
"go_register_toolchains")
go_rules_dependencies()
go_register_toolchains()
```

Save your WORKSPACE file.

For this particular example, we are going to put all of our code into a single directory. In practice, you will likely want to separate out the code by language for the sake of organization.

Now let's create a directory for our work and an accompanying BUILD file:

```
chapter_05$ mkdir src
chapter_05$ cd src
chapter_05/src$ touch BUILD
```

As you have seen previously, some languages (e.g., C++, Java, etc.) come out of the box with Bazel; as such, we don't need to explicitly load in those rules. However, as you saw in the previous chapter, we need to explicitly load the rules for other languages. In this case, we are going to load in the Go rules.

Open the BUILD file and add the following.

Listing 5-2. Loading the Go language rules

```
load("@io_bazel_rules_go//go:def.bzl", "go_library", "go_binary")
```

Save your BUILD file.

Now let's create some programs. We will start with the Go version.

Go Echo Server

We will start with a simple Go echo server. As the name implies, its main job is to accept incoming connections, read the bytes off the connection, and return a (modified) version of the same bytes back.

Listing 5-3. Simple Go echo server

```go
package main

import (
    "log"
    "net"
)

func main() {
    log.Println("Spinning up the Echo Server in Go...")
    listen, error := net.Listen("tcp", ":1234")
    if error != nil {
        log.Panicln("Unable to listen: " + error.Error())
    }
    defer listen.Close()

    connection, error := listen.Accept()
    if error != nil {
        log.Panicln("Cannot accept a connection! Error: " + error.Error())
    }

    log.Println("Receiving on a new connection")
    defer connection.Close()
    defer log.Println("Connection now closed.")

    buffer := make([]byte, 2048)
    size, error := connection.Read(buffer)
    if error != nil {
        log.Println("Cannot read from the buffer! Error: " + error.Error())
    }
    data := string(buffer[:size])
    log.Println("Received data: " + data)
    connection.Write([]byte("Echoed from Go: " + data))
}
```

Save this to chapter_05/src/echo_server.go.

Just to walk through the code a bit, the Go echo server will start listening for connections on port "1234." Once it has accepted a connection, it will read off the data from that connection, modify it slightly (i.e., prepending "Echoed from Go:"), and then send that modified data back to the sender. For the sake of simplicity, once it has echoed the data, it will close up shop.

Now let's create the entry within the BUILD file for the build target.

Listing 5-4. Go echo server build target

```
go_binary(
    name = "echo_server",
    srcs = ["echo_server.go"],
)
```

Save the BUILD file.

Now it's time to actually build and run the echo server:

```
chapter_05/src$ bazel run :echo_server
INFO: Analysed target //src:echo_server (0 packages loaded, 0 targets
     configured).
INFO: Found 1 target...
Target //src:echo_server up-to-date:
  bazel-bin/src/darwin_amd64_stripped/echo_server
INFO: Elapsed time: 0.125s, Critical Path: 0.00s
INFO: 0 processes.
INFO: Build completed successfully, 1 total action
INFO: Build completed successfully, 1 total action
2019/06/02 17:49:07 Spinning up the Echo Server in Go...
```

At this point, it is going to just be hanging around forever, since it has no one to connect to it. Kill the process and let's fix that. We'll be putting down Go for a moment and jumping over to the Java.

Java Echo Client

As the name implies, we will be creating a program to connect to our echo server. The echo client will attempt to connect to the server, read in some data from the user, transmit that to the server, and then write out whatever it gets back from the server.

Listing 5-5. Simple Java echo client

```java
import java.io.BufferedReader;
import java.io.InputStreamReader;
import java.io.PrintWriter;
import java.net.Socket;

public class EchoClient {
    public static void main (String args[]) {
        System.out.println("Spinning up the Echo Client in Java...");
        try {
            final Socket socketToServer = new Socket("localhost", 1234);
            final BufferedReader inputFromServer = new BufferedReader(
                new InputStreamReader(socketToServer.getInputStream()));
            final BufferedReader commandLineInput = new BufferedReader(
                new InputStreamReader(System.in));

            System.out.println("Waiting on input from the user...");
            final String inputFromUser = commandLineInput.readLine();
            if (inputFromUser != null) {
                System.out.println("Received by Java: " + inputFromUser);
                final PrintWriter outputToServer =
                    new PrintWriter(socketToServer.getOutputStream(), true);
                outputToServer.println(inputFromUser);
                System.out.println(inputFromServer.readLine());
            }
            socketToServer.close();
        } catch (Exception e) {
            System.err.println("Error: " + e);
        }
    }
}
```

Save the preceding code to the file chapter_05/src/EchoClient.java.

The EchoClient attempts to create a local connection to a server on port 1234. Assuming success, it then reads a single line of data from the user, sends it over the connection, and prints the response from the server. Once again, for the sake of simplicity, this will run only once and then shut down.

Now let's add its entry into the BUILD file.

Listing 5-6. Java echo client build target

```
java_binary(
    name = "EchoClient",
    srcs = ["EchoClient.java"],
)
```

Save this to the BUILD file.

Let's run this on its own to make sure that we can build and run:

```
chapter_05/src$ bazel run :EchoClient
INFO: Analysed target //src:EchoClient (0 packages loaded, 2 targets
      configured).
INFO: Found 1 target...
Target //src:EchoClient up-to-date:
  bazel-bin/src/EchoClient.jar
  bazel-bin/src/EchoClient
INFO: Elapsed time: 0.342s, Critical Path: 0.12s
INFO: 1 process: 1 worker.
INFO: Build completed successfully, 2 total actions
INFO: Build completed successfully, 2 total actions
Spinning up the Echo Client in Java...
Error: java.net.ConnectException: Connection refused (Connection refused)
```

Congratulations! Your program successfully runs... and then terminates because there is nothing to connect to. No worries, we will correct this in a moment.

Naming the Echo Client and Server

An astute reader would notice that the name of our Java target has a different style from the name in our Go target.

Specifically, we have one name formed primarily through underscores and one through camel casing.

Listing 5-7. Build targets

```
go_binary(
    name = "echo_server",
    srcs = ["echo_server.go"],
)

java_binary(
    name = "EchoClient",
    srcs = ["EchoClient.java"],
)
```

To be clear, this is not an editorial mistake in this case; there is actually some reason to the difference, at least for Java. For the Java binary build target, the name of the target is also used as a shorthand to inform Bazel what is the main class within the set of sources.

To illustrate, let's modify the name of the java_binary build target to match the style of the go_binary build target.

Listing 5-8. Modified java_binary name style

```
java_binary(
    name = "echo_client",
    srcs = ["EchoClient.java"],
)
```

Save this change to the BUILD file.

Building still works as expected:

```
chapter_05/src$ bazel build :echo_client
INFO: Analysed target //src:echo_client (1 packages loaded, 2 targets
    configured).
INFO: Found 1 target...
Target //src:echo_client up-to-date:
  bazel-bin/src/echo_client.jar
  bazel-bin/src/echo_client
INFO: Elapsed time: 0.261s, Critical Path: 0.09s
INFO: 1 process: 1 worker.
INFO: Build completed successfully, 3 total actions
```

However, you will find that you cannot actually run the program:

```
chapter_05/src$ bazel run :echo_client
INFO: Analysed target //src:echo_client (0 packages loaded, 0 targets
      configured).
INFO: Found 1 target...
Target //src:echo_client up-to-date:
  bazel-bin/src/echo_client.jar
  bazel-bin/src/echo_client
INFO: Elapsed time: 0.137s, Critical Path: 0.00s
INFO: 0 processes.
INFO: Build completed successfully, 1 total action
INFO: Build completed successfully, 1 total action
Error: Could not find or load main class echo_client
```

Without any additional guidance, the java_binary rule makes use of the name of the build target to infer the class in which the main function lives (or more to the point, the class whose main function *should* be used). In our modified case, Bazel is attempting to find the class echo_client, which does not exist.

This outcome should make sense. Although the Bazel rule has a convenience to elide the specification of the main class with the build target's name, failing that convention, it will not attempt to implicitly select a class with a potential main class. As illustrated, this is even in the case where there is only one class.

Fortunately, we can add an explicit declaration to make things work again.

Listing 5-9. Explicitly listing the java_binary main class

```
java_binary(
    name = "echo_client",
    srcs = ["EchoClient.java"],
    main_class = "EchoClient",
)
```

Save this change to the BUILD file.

Running will now work as before:

```
chapter_05/src$ bazel run :echo_client
INFO: Analysed target //src:echo_client (1 packages loaded, 2 targets
      configured).
INFO: Found 1 target...
Target //src:echo_client up-to-date:
  bazel-bin/src/echo_client.jar
  bazel-bin/src/echo_client
INFO: Elapsed time: 0.204s, Critical Path: 0.00s
INFO: 0 processes.
INFO: Build completed successfully, 2 total actions
INFO: Build completed successfully, 2 total actions
Spinning up the Echo Client in Java...
Error: java.net.ConnectException: Connection refused (Connection refused)
```

The preceding code is a reminder that Bazel wants everything as explicit as possible. True, some of the rules do provide some shortcuts to make life easier, but ultimately Bazel does not want dependency management or build specification to be "magical." By making our dependencies, build specifications, and so on explicit, Bazel is able to perform optimizations and guarantees to make our builds fast, stable, and well understood.

Now, let's actually run our programs together.

Echoing Between Programs

Having created our client and our server programs, now it is time to run them together. You will need two different instances of your shell to run each of these.

Within your first shell, let's get the server back up and running:

```
chapter_05/src$ bazel run :echo_server
INFO: Analysed target //src:echo_server (0 packages loaded, 2 targets
      configured).
INFO: Found 1 target...
Target //src:echo_server up-to-date:
  bazel-bin/src/darwin_amd64_stripped/echo_server
INFO: Elapsed time: 0.210s, Critical Path: 0.00s
INFO: 0 processes.
```

```
INFO: Build completed successfully, 1 total action
INFO: Build completed successfully, 1 total action
2019/06/02 18:50:31 Spinning up the Echo Server in Go...
```

That will hold until it actually gets a connection; let's provide one. Open your second shell and run the client program:

```
chapter_05/src$ bazel run :echo_client
INFO: Analysed target //src:echo_client (0 packages loaded, 0 targets
      configured).
INFO: Found 1 target...
Target //src:echo_client up-to-date:
  bazel-bin/src/echo_client.jar
  bazel-bin/src/echo_client
INFO: Elapsed time: 0.284s, Critical Path: 0.00s
INFO: 0 processes.
INFO: Build completed successfully, 1 total action
INFO: Build completed successfully, 1 total action
Spinning up the Echo Client in Java...
Waiting on input from the user...
```

Now, just enter in some text that you want to send and press *enter*. In your second shell (the client), you should have something like this:

```
chapter_05/src$ bazel run :echo_client
<omitted from above>
Spinning up the Echo Client in Java...
Waiting on input from the user...
Hello, friends!
Received by Java: Hello, friends!
Echoed from Go: Hello, friends!
```

The client program should have also cleanly exited.

Looking at your first shell (the server), you should have something like this:

```
chapter_05/src$ bazel run :echo_server
<omitted from above>
2019/06/02 18:50:31 Spinning up the Echo Server in Go...
```

```
2019/06/02 18:52:28 Receiving on a new connection
2019/06/02 18:53:25 Received data: Hello, friends!
2019/06/02 18:53:25 Connection now closed.
```

As with the client, your server should now have also cleanly exited. Congratulations! You have created an echo client and server in different languages in Bazel!

Upgrading to JSON

Sending byte strings back and forth is a good start, but it is not a scalable way to send messages. In this section, we will pivot over to using JSON to transmit data over the data connection. In the process, we will tie together some concepts we have been building over the last few chapters.

For the sake of illustration, we will construct a simple JSON message, which has the following data.

Listing 5-10. Simple JSON message

```
{
  "message": "This is my message",
  "value": 1234.56
}
```

JSON in Go

Go provides out-of-the-box support for marshaling and unmarshaling data between JSON and an instance of a Go struct. First, we will create a Go struct to define the transmission message.

For the most part, we need only create a plain data struct in Go with the necessary fields. The only small change is that we need to add some annotation to specify the mapping of the JSON key to the particular member of the struct.

Listing 5-11. Simple JSON object in Go

```
package transmission_object

type TransmissionObject struct {
    Message string `json:"message"`
    Value   float32 `json:"value"`
}
```

Within the `chapter_05/src` directory, save the preceding file to `transmission_object.go`.

Now let's create a `go_library` in the `BUILD` file to provide a build target for this functionality. Open the `chapter_05/src/BUILD` file and add the following to it.

Listing 5-12. Adding the TransmissionObject as a go_library

```
go_library(
    name = "transmission_object_go",
    srcs = ["transmission_object.go"],
    importpath = "transmission_object",
)
```

Save the *BUILD* file

Now, let's add the necessary functionality within your Go echo server. In this case, we will read the incoming message, make a bit of modification to the values within the message, and then send the modified message back.

Open `echo_server.go` and add the following lines.

Listing 5-13. Unmarshaling, modifying, and marshaling a JSON object in Go

```
package main

import (
    "encoding/json"
    "fmt"
    "log"
    "net"
    "transmission_object"
)
```

```go
func main() {
<omitted from above>

        data := buffer[:size]
        var transmissionObject transmission_object.TransmissionObject
        error = json.Unmarshal(data, &transmissionObject)
        if error != nil {
                log.Panicln(
                        "Unable to unmarshal the buffer! Error: " +
                        error.Error())
        }

        log.Println("Message = " + transmissionObject.Message)
        log.Println("Value = " + fmt.Sprintf("%f", transmissionObject.Value))

        transmissionObject.Message =
                "Echoed from Go: " + transmissionObject.Message
        transmissionObject.Value = 2 * transmissionObject.Value

        message, error := json.Marshal(transmissionObject)
        if error != nil {
                log.Panicln(
                        "Unable to marshall the object! Error: " +
                        error.Error())
        }
        connection.Write(message)
}
```

Save the changes to chapter_05/src/echo_server.go.

Finally, we need to update the BUILD file to have the correct dependencies for echo_server. Open the BUILD file and make the following changes.

Listing 5-14. Updating the BUILD file

```
go_binary(
    name = "echo_server",
    srcs = ["echo_server.go"],
    deps = [":transmission_object_go"],
)
```

Save the changes to `chapter_05/src/BUILD`.

Now let's move onto the `echo_client` to make the necessary changes.

JSON in Java

Go has built-in facilities for transforming JSON into instances of Go structs; Java, unfortunately, does not have the same capabilities out of the box. Fortunately, we can acquire similar behavior by using the GSON library.

GSON Setup

Back in Chapter 3, you downloaded a jar file to the `third_party` directory; here we will do the same again, this time to retrieve the GSON library.

First, create the `third_party/gson` directory:

```
chapter_05$ mkdir third_party
chapter_05$ cd third_party
chapter_05/third_party$ mkdir gson
```

Download the JAR from the following location:

`http://central.maven.org/maven2/com/google/code/gson/gson/2.8.5/gson--2.8.5.jar`.

Copy the JAR file to the `third_party/gson` directory. As before, we now create the BUILD file for the external dependency.

Listing 5-15. Contents of the BUILD file for the third_party dependency

```
package(default_visibility = ["//visibility:public"])

java_import(
 name = "gson",
 jars = ["gson/gson-2.8.5.jar"]
)
```

Save the BUILD file to the `third_party` directory.

Adding the Transmission Object to EchoClient

Now we will create a `TransmissionObject` in Java (equivalent to what we did in Go) for sending and receiving structured and typed info over the wire.

Listing 5-16. Transmission Object in Java

```
public class TransmissionObject {
    public String message;
    public float value;
}
```

Save the preceding code to `chapter_05/src/TransmissionObject.java`. Now let's update the BUILD file with a new `java_library` build target for this object.

Listing 5-17. Updating the BUILD file

```
java_library(
    name = "transmission_object_java",
    srcs = ["TransmissionObject.java"],
)
```

Save the changes to `chapter_05/src/BUILD`.

Now let's add the changes to `EchoClient.java` to marshal the data, send the message, and then print out the response from the echo server.

Listing 5-18. Adding transmission to the echo client

```
import com.google.gson.Gson;
import com.google.gson.GsonBuilder;

<omitted from above>

    System.out.println("Waiting on input from the user...");
    final String inputFromUser = commandLineInput.readLine();
    if (inputFromUser != null) {
        System.out.println("Received by Java: " + inputFromUser);

        TransmissionObject transmissionObject =
            new TransmissionObject();
```

```
        transmissionObject.message = inputFromUser;
        transmissionObject.value = 3.145f;
        GsonBuilder builder = new GsonBuilder();
        Gson gson = builder.create();
        final PrintWriter outputToServer =
            new PrintWriter(socketToServer.getOutputStream(), true);
        outputToServer.println(gson.toJson(transmissionObject));
        System.out.println(inputFromServer.readLine());
    }
    socketToServer.close();
}
```

Save the preceding code to chapter_05/src/EchoClient.java. Finally, we can now add the necessary updates to the BUILD file.

Listing 5-19. Updating the Java client with the new dependencies

```
java_binary(
 name = "echo_client",
 srcs = ["EchoClient.java"],
 main_class = "EchoClient",
 deps = [
     ":transmission_object_java",
     "//third_party:gson",
 ]
)
```

Save the preceding code to chapter_05/src/BUILD.

Executing the Echo Client/Server with JSON

With all the pieces in place, let's run the server and the client. Once again, you will need two terminal instances in order to properly the run the client and server.

First, we will run the echo server:

```
chapter_05/src$ bazel run :echo_server
INFO: Analysed target //src:echo_server (0 packages loaded, 0 targets
      configured).
INFO: Found 1 target...
Target //src:echo_server up-to-date:
  bazel-bin/src/darwin_amd64_stripped/echo_server
INFO: Elapsed time: 0.132s, Critical Path: 0.00s
INFO: 0 processes.
INFO: Build completed successfully, 1 total action
INFO: Build completed successfully, 1 total action
2019/06/04 00:27:23 Spinning up the Echo Server in Go...
```

In the second terminal instance, we will run the echo client:

```
chapter_05/src$ bazel run :echo_client
INFO: Analysed target //src:echo_client (0 packages loaded, 0 targets
      configured).
INFO: Found 1 target...
Target //src:echo_client up-to-date:
  bazel-bin/src/echo_client.jar
  bazel-bin/src/echo_client
INFO: Elapsed time: 0.115s, Critical Path: 0.00s
INFO: 0 processes.
INFO: Build completed successfully, 1 total action
INFO: Build completed successfully, 1 total action
Spinning up the Echo Client in Java...
Waiting on input from the user...
```

Let's add the user input:

```
chapter_05/src$ bazel run :echo_client
<omitted from above>
Spinning up the Echo Client in Java...
Waiting on input from the user...
My Client Message
{"message":"Echoed from Go: My Client Message","value":6.29}
```

Finally, let's look at the console output from the echo server:

```
chapter_05/src$ bazel run :echo_server
<omitted from above>
2019/06/04 00:27:23 Spinning up the Echo Server in Go...
2019/06/04 00:29:08 Receiving on a new connection
2019/06/04 00:30:04 Message = My Client Message
2019/06/04 00:30:04 Value = 3.145000
```

Congratulations! You have successfully augmented your client and server programs for transmitting JSON data between different languages.

Final Word: Duplication of Effort

One unfortunate reality of using JSON is that we need to duplicate the data definitions for each language. Should the data contract change, this means that every instance of the data definition needs to be changed. This is an error-prone process and, while better than simple strings transmission, still has a number of shortcomings.

As stated previously, one of the areas that Bazel excels is in multi-language support; in the next chapter, we are going to lean into this capability as we add Protocol Buffer support to our project.

EXERCISE – PYTHON CLIENT AND/OR SERVER

As with Go, Python has some handy capabilities for marshaling to/from Python objects from JSON. Create either a new client or a server in Python.

CHAPTER 6

Protocol Buffers and Bazel

In the last chapter, you created a simple echo server and client, demonstrating some of the power of Bazel to navigate and manage multiple languages with minimal setup. A noted shortcoming from that example stems from the definition of the transmitted object: both languages required independent definitions of the object. Over time, this easily can cause a literal breakdown in communication as two (or more) definitions of the transmitted object drift out of sync.

In this chapter, we are going to introduce a construct to handle this very problem, the *Protocol Buffer* (often referred to as *protobuf*). Yet another creation from Google, Protocol Buffers provide a way to describe the structure of objects in a declarative and type-safe fashion and provide a wire format for serialization. Protocol Buffer definitions are intrinsically language agnostic. Once created, a Protocol Buffer definition can then be compiled into a particular language (there is vast language support for Protocol Buffers) in order to read/write from the wire format into a language native object.

While Protocol Buffers are not wedded to Bazel per se, Bazel provides some fantastic support for them, making it easy to add them to a project and make use of them across multiple languages. In addition, due to Bazel's dependency management, it is also very easy to make a change at the Protocol Buffer definition and ensure that all the dependent projects can at least compile against the new definition.

© P.J. McNerney 2020
P.J. McNerney, *Beginning Bazel*, https://doi.org/10.1007/978-1-4842-5194-2_6

Setting Up Your Workspace

We will start first with adding some very basic support to a WORKSPACE file for working with Protocol Buffers. Let's create a new directory for our work:

```
$ mkdir chapter_06
$ cd chapter_06
chapter_06$ touch WORKSPACE
```

Now let's pull in the rules for working with Protocol Buffers. Open your WORKSPACE file and add the following.

Listing 6-1. Adding support for Protocol Buffers

```
http_archive(
    name = "rules_proto",
    strip_prefix = "rules_proto-97d8af4dc474595af3900dd85cb3a29ad28cc313",
    urls = ["https://github.com/bazelbuild/rules_proto/archive/97d8af4dc474
        595af3900dd85cb3a29ad28cc313.tar.gz",],
)
load("@rules_proto//proto:repositories.bzl", "rules_proto_dependencies",
"rules_proto_toolchains")
rules_proto_dependencies()
rules_proto_toolchains()
```

Save your WORKSPACE file.

As should be familiar from prior chapters, we are first retrieving the Bazel repository with the required functionality and then calling setup code particular to that repository (i.e., rules_proto_dependencies() and rules_proto_toolchains()).

Creating Your First Protocol Buffer

Having completed setup, we are ready to start creating some Protocol Buffers. Let's create a directory for our code and an initial file for our Protocol Buffer definition:

```
chapter_06$ mkdir src
chapter_06$ cd src
chapter_06/src$ touch transmission_object.proto
```

Note   An astute reader will note that in the prior chapter, we had started off with creating our BUILD file before working with the code. This switch here is intentional, and we will address it very shortly.

Let's create a basic message for transmission. Open your transmission_object.proto file and add the following.

Listing 6-2. Defining a simple Protocol Buffer

```
syntax = "proto3";

package transmission_object;

message TransmissionObject {
    float value = 1;
    string message = 2;
}
```

Save that to transmission_object.proto.

Let's take a brief moment to examine what we have written. The initial line (syntax) is used to specify to the compiler what version of Protocol Buffers is being used here (at the time of this writing, the latest version of Protocol Buffers is version 3).

The following line (package) is used to define the conceptual package that this Protocol Buffer is defined within. This is very similar to the Java or Go notions of packages.

Finally, we have the definition of the message itself. This most closely resembles a C-style struct, with a name given to the object (TransmissionObject) and a basic set of type-specified fields (i.e., value and message, with types float and string, respectively). The one minor addition here is the addition of a field number; this is used to define unique identifiers to each of the members of the message. This is important since these are used to add and remove data members while keeping backward compatibility.

Now let's create the build target for the Protocol Buffer. Add the following to your BUILD file.

Listing 6-3. Creating the build target for the Protocol Buffer

```
load("@rules_proto//proto:defs.bzl", "proto_library")
proto_library(
    name = "transmission_object_proto",
    srcs = ["transmission_object.proto"],
)
```

Save your BUILD file.

Note   Those already familiar with Bazel might find the explicit inclusion of proto_library to be strange. The proto_library rule used to be a part of the core of Bazel itself. This is an example of the evolution of Bazel by moving specific constructs out of the core and into explicit packages.

At this stage, we technically have enough to start building our Protocol Buffer, so let's do that:

```
chapter_06/src$ bazel build :transmission_object_proto
INFO: Analysed target //src:transmission_object_proto (16 packages loaded,
    624 targets configured).
INFO: Found 1 target...
Target //src:transmission_object_proto up-to-date:
  bazel-genfiles/src/transmission_object_proto-descriptor-set.proto.bin
INFO: Elapsed time: 80.442s, Critical Path: 24.91s
INFO: 184 processes: 184 darwin-sandbox.
INFO: Build completed successfully, 187 total actions
```

One of the first things that you should notice is that, for at least the first time you build the Protocol Buffer target, there is a noticeable delay compared to executions in prior chapters. In this case, the dependency for the Protocol Buffer compiler is both being pulled down *and* being compiled for your target machine. Once the protobuf compiler is itself compiled, then it can then compile your protobuf definition.

Don't worry. This particular slowdown should only be limited to the first time you actually run the Protocol Buffer compiler; once created, the Protocol Buffer compiler will remain cached (until you change a dependency or execute bazel clean).

Using the Protocol Buffer in Java

Although we have successfully compiled the Protocol Buffer, all we really have done is create a language-agnostic descriptor for it; in order to really make use of it, we will need to create a language-specific target for it. We will start with creating one in Java. Once again, we take advantage of the fact that Java, being one of the built-in languages of Bazel, comes with support built-in for Java-based Protocol Buffers.

Creating the Java Proto Library Target

Open your BUILD file and add the following.

Listing 6-4. Creating the Java Protocol Buffer library

```
java_proto_library(
    name = "transmission_object_java_proto",
    deps = [":transmission_object_proto"],
)
```

Save the BUILD file. Let's build the newly created target:

```
chapter_06/src$ bazel build :transmission_object_java_proto
INFO: Analysed target //src:transmission_object_java_proto (2 packages
    loaded, 350 targets configured).
INFO: Found 1 target...
Target //src:transmission_object_java_proto up-to-date:
  bazel-bin/src/libtransmission_object_proto-speed.jar
  bazel-genfiles/src/transmission_object_proto-speed-src.jar
INFO: Elapsed time: 0.703s, Critical Path: 0.45s
INFO: 2 processes: 1 darwin-sandbox, 1 worker.
INFO: Build completed successfully, 3 total actions
```

Congratulations! You have a target that we can actually use in a Java program.

Note   In this case, you did not need to explicitly load `java_proto_library`. However, given Bazel's evolution, bear in mind that some future iteration may require you to explicitly load the rule.

Using Your Java Protocol Buffer Target

In the last chapter, you had created a simple Java echo client using JSON. Here, we will make use of almost the same code for the Protocol Buffer example, with only a few minor changes.

Create EchoClient.java within your src directory and add the following (changes from the prior chapter in bold).

Listing 6-5. Protocol Buffer version of the echo client

```java
import java.io.BufferedReader;
import java.io.InputStreamReader;
import java.io.PrintWriter;
import java.net.Socket;

import transmission_object.TransmissionObjectOuterClass.TransmissionObject;

public class EchoClient {
    public static void main (String args[]) {
        System.out.println("Spinning up the Echo Client in Java...");
        try {
            final Socket socketToServer = new Socket("localhost", 1234);
            // Note we don't need the second BufferedReader here.
            final BufferedReader commandLineInput = new BufferedReader
            (new InputStreamReader(System.in));

            System.out.println("Waiting on input from the user...");
            final String inputFromUser = commandLineInput.readLine();
            if (inputFromUser != null) {
                System.out.println("Received by Java: " + inputFromUser);
                TransmissionObject transmissionObject = TransmissionObject.
                  newBuilder()
                    .setMessage(inputFromUser)
                    .setValue(3.145f)
                    .build();
                transmissionObject.writeTo(socketToServer.getOutputStream());
                TransmissionObject receivedObject = TransmissionObject.
                parseFrom(socketToServer.getInputStream());
```

```
            System.out.println("Received Message from server: ");
            System.out.println(receivedObject);
        }
        socketToServer.close();
    } catch (Exception e) {
        System.err.println("Error: " + e);
    }
  }
}
```

Save this to EchoClient.java.

Let's take a moment to examine the preceding code. The import statement that brings in our generated Protocol Buffer is comprised of three main components:

- transmission_object

    - This is the package as specified within the original transmission_object.proto file.

- TransmissionObjectOuterClass

    - This is a class generated to encapsulate any messages contained within the Protocol Buffer definition.

    - This is an artifact of Java's one (outer)-class-per-file rule; technically, we could have had multiple messages within our Protocol Buffer file, but we can only have a single class within a Java file.

    - This allows us to create multiple Protocol Buffer messages for use in Java.

- TransmissionObject

    - The actual Java object that represents the original Protocol Buffer message.

Within the code itself, the Java Protocol Buffer instance is created using a builder pattern, which allows you to set the various fields and then generate an invariant instance of the TransmissionObject. This object is then able to directly write itself to an output stream as well as parse itself from an input stream.

Finally, let's create the build target so we can actually create our new version of EchoClient. Open your BUILD file and add the following (again, changes from last chapter in bold).

Listing 6-6. Creating the BUILD target for the EchoClient

```
java_binary(
    name = "echo_client",
    srcs = ["EchoClient.java"],
    main_class = "EchoClient",
    deps = [":transmission_object_java_proto"],
)
```

Now we can build the target:

```
chapter_06/src$ bazel build :echo_client
INFO: Analysed target //src:echo_client (0 packages loaded, 0 targets
      configured).
INFO: Found 1 target...
Target //src:echo_client up-to-date:
  bazel-bin/src/echo_client.jar
  bazel-bin/src/echo_client
INFO: Elapsed time: 0.219s, Critical Path: 0.06s
INFO: 1 process: 1 worker.
INFO: Build completed successfully, 2 total actions
```

Congratulations! You've successfully updated your client to use Protocol Buffers. However, once again you have a client with nothing to connect to. Now, we will make the necessary changes to the server side to also handle our Protocol Buffer definition.

Note   One might be tempted to run this new version of our client against the last chapter's server. Although you are welcome to do so, it is important to know that this will not work, since the client and server are talking into different protocols (JSON vs. Protocol Buffer); the bytes are going to be interpreted differently.

Although Protocol Buffers *do* support translation to/from JSON, you would need to explicitly specify that within the code.

Using the Protocol Buffer in Go

In the last section, we were able to take advantage of the fact that Java is one of the built-in languages of Bazel to jump right into development. However, since Go is *not* one of those core languages, we will need to do some additional setup. Fortunately, most of this will look familiar from prior chapters.

Open your WORKSPACE file and add the following in bold prior to the specification for retrieving rules_proto.

Listing 6-7. Adding the Go rules to the project

```
http_archive(
    name = "io_bazel_rules_go",
    urls = ["https://github.com/bazelbuild/rules_go/releases/download/
            v0.19.5/rules_go-v0.19.5.tar.gz"],
)
load("@io_bazel_rules_go//go:deps.bzl", "go_rules_dependencies",
"go_register_toolchains")
go_rules_dependencies()
go_register_toolchains()

http_archive(
    name = "rules_proto",
    strip_prefix = "rules_proto-97d8af4dc474595af3900dd85cb3a29ad28cc313",
    urls = ["https://github.com/bazelbuild/rules_proto/archive/97d8af4dc474
            595af3900dd85cb3a29ad28cc313.tar.gz",],
)
load("@rules_proto//proto:repositories.bzl", "rules_proto_dependencies",
"rules_proto_toolchains")
rules_proto_dependencies()
rules_proto_toolchains()
```

Save your *WORKSPACE* file.j

> **Note**   In this particular instance, we specified to load `io_bazel_rules_go` prior
> to `rules_proto`. The reason is that there can be conflicts between the underlying
> dependencies between these two packages. Ordering them in this fashion
> removes the issue. However, this is an item to watch out for as you construct your
> WORKSPACE dependencies moving forward.

Creating the Go Proto Library Target

As with the inclusion of the Go functionality into our project, we will need to explicitly
bring the necessary rules into our BUILD file as we create our Go proto library target.

Open your BUILD file and add the following.

Listing 6-8.   Creating the Go proto library target

```
load("@io_bazel_rules_go//proto:def.bzl", "go_proto_library")
go_proto_library(
    name = "transmission_object_go_proto",
    proto = ":transmission_object_proto",
    importpath = "transmission_object"
)
```

Save your BUILD file. Let's build your new target:

```
chapter_06/src$ bazel build :transmission_object_go_proto
INFO: Analysed target //src:transmission_object_go_proto (21 packages
    loaded, 6358 targets configured).
INFO: Found 1 target...
...
Target //src:transmission_object_go_proto up-to-date:
  bazel-bin/src/darwin_amd64_stripped/transmission_object_go_proto%/
transmission_object.a
INFO: Elapsed time: 5.486s, Critical Path: 3.75s
INFO: 52 processes: 52 darwin-sandbox.
INFO: Build completed successfully, 54 total actions
```

As with your prior experience when creating the Java Protocol Buffer target, you likely will notice a slightly longer-than-normal build time. Once again, this is normal, since the language-specific (i.e., Go) plug-in is being compiled; as before, after the first time, this is cached, and later builds will go much quicker.

Once again, congratulations, since we now have a target that we can actually use in our Go program. Now let's modify our echo server to take advantage of this.

Using Your Go Protocol Buffer Target

As with the echo client, in the last chapter, you had created a version of the echo server that bounced back the received JSON message (with some modifications). As before, we are going to be able to make some slight changes to our original program to handle Protocol Buffers.

Create the file echo_server.go in src and add the following to it (as before, changes from the prior chapter in bold).

Listing 6-9. Protocol Buffer version of the Go server

```
package main

import (
        "fmt"
        "log"
        "net"
        "transmission_object"
        "github.com/golang/protobuf/proto"
)

func main() {
        log.Println("Spinning up the Echo Server in Go...")
        listen, error := net.Listen("tcp", ":1234")
        if error != nil {
                log.Panicln("Unable to listen: " + error.Error())
        }
        defer listen.Close()

        connection, error := listen.Accept()
        if error != nil {
```

```go
        log.Panicln("Cannot accept a connection! Error: " + error.
        Error())
}

log.Println("Receiving on a new connection")
defer connection.Close()
defer log.Println("Connection now closed.")

buffer := make([]byte, 2048)
size, error := connection.Read(buffer)
if error != nil {
        log.Panicln(
            "Unable to read from the buffer! Error: " + error.Error())
}
data := buffer[:size]
transmissionObject := &transmission_object.TransmissionObject{}
error = proto.Unmarshal(data, transmissionObject)
if error != nil {
        log.Panicln(
            "Unable to unmarshal the buffer! Error: " + error.Error())
}

log.Println("Message = " + transmissionObject.GetMessage())
log.Println("Value = " +
    fmt.Sprintf("%f", transmissionObject.GetValue()))

transmissionObject.Message = "Echoed from Go: " +
    transmissionObject.GetMessage()
transmissionObject.Value = 2 * transmissionObject.GetValue()

message, error := proto.Marshal(transmissionObject)
if error != nil {
        log.Panicln("Unable to marshal the object! Error: " + error.
        Error())
}
connection.Write(message)
}
```

Save this to echo_server.go.

While the changes are not a complete drop-in replacement for the JSON, the final result is extremely close to what we had in the previous chapter.

Of particular note, we have to bring in a dependency on the proto library itself (github.com/golang/protobuf/proto) in order to perform the unmarshaling/marshaling of the object from/to the data streams. Unlike the previous dependency on the encoding package in Go, we will need to account for this when we specify the dependencies within the BUILD file.

Open the BUILD file and add the following to create the necessary build target (differences from the last chapter in bold).

Listing 6-10. Adding the echo server build target

```
load("@io_bazel_rules_go//go:def.bzl", "go_binary")
go_binary(
    name = "echo_server",
    srcs = ["echo_server.go"],
    deps = [
        ":transmission_object_go_proto",
        "@com_github_golang_protobuf//proto:go_default_library",
    ],
)
```

Save your BUILD file.

DEPENDENCIES FROM DEPENDENCIES

An astute reader will notice that the dependency we have specified for the go_default_library is not actually specified within the WORKSPACE file; however, the preceding code still compiles without complaint.

The source of this additional dependency stems from the function that we called to set up the additional dependencies for the Go rules (i.e., go_rules_dependencies), which pulled in additional dependencies, including the above-listed one.

Although technically this is "explicitly" specified within the WORKSPACE file, it is obfuscated by the use of the dependencies function. In this case, we are taking advantage of the fact that all of these versions of the particular dependencies are meant to work in concert.

If this is too implicit, then a couple things can be done: (1) Explicitly specify a dependency within the WORKSPACE file; this will replace the version of the implicit dependency. (2) Pull the dependency into your project (e.g., through a third_party directory).

The decision on which route to pursues relates to how tightly you want to control your dependencies. (1) may be easier as a way to quickly get up and running and make it easier to change dependencies later on. However, again, (2) provides the strongest guarantee for build reproducibility.

Now we can build our echo server with Protocol Buffer support:

```
chapter_06/src$ bazel build :echo_server
INFO: Analysed target //src:echo_server (0 packages loaded, 0 targets
     configured).
INFO: Found 1 target...
Target //src:echo_server up-to-date:
  bazel-bin/src/darwin_amd64_stripped/echo_server
INFO: Elapsed time: 0.169s, Critical Path: 0.00s
INFO: 0 processes.
INFO: Build completed successfully, 1 total action
```

Echo Using Protocol Buffers

Having reconstructed our echo client and server with Protocol Buffers, we are now ready to have them start talking to each other again.

Open a terminal and start running the server:

```
chapter_06/src$ bazel run :echo_server
INFO: Analysed target //src:echo_server (0 packages loaded, 0 targets
     configured).
INFO: Found 1 target...
Target //src:echo_server up-to-date:
  bazel-bin/src/darwin_amd64_stripped/echo_server
INFO: Elapsed time: 0.169s, Critical Path: 0.00s
INFO: 0 processes.
INFO: Build completed successfully, 1 total action
INFO: Build completed successfully, 1 total action
2019/06/18 23:39:53 Spinning up the Echo Server in Go...
```

Now let's open a separate terminal and start up the client:

```
chapter_06/src$ bazel run :echo_client
INFO: Analysed target //src:echo_client (0 packages loaded, 0 targets
      configured).
INFO: Found 1 target...
Target //src:echo_client up-to-date:
  bazel-bin/src/echo_client.jar
  bazel-bin/src/echo_client
INFO: Elapsed time: 0.249s, Critical Path: 0.10s
INFO: 1 process: 1 worker.
INFO: Build completed successfully, 2 total actions
INFO: Build completed successfully, 2 total actions
Spinning up the Echo Client in Java...
Waiting on input from the user...
```

Now, let's give it a little bit of text:

```
chapter_06/src$ bazel run :echo_client
<omitted from above>
Spinning up the Echo Client in Java...
Waiting on input from the user...
Waiting on input from the user...
My Client Message
Received by Java: My Client Message
Received Message from server:
value: 6.29
message: "Echoed from Go: My Client Message"
```

Now let's check out the console output from the echo server:

```
chapter_06/src$ bazel run :echo_server
<omitted from above>
2019/06/18 23:41:50 Receiving on a new connection
2019/06/18 23:43:34 Message = My Client Message
2019/06/18 23:43:34 Value = 3.145000
2019/06/18 23:43:34 Connection now closed.
```

Congratulations! You've recreated the echo client/server using Protocol Buffers.

Dependency Tracking and Management

Compared to the previous chapter, there are some slight formatting differences, but the outputs are effectively the same. This begs an obvious question: Why did we reinvent everything from the last chapter? The answer lies in how we manage changes to our selected transmission object; this, in turn, showcases the ability of Bazel to perform dependency management, even across multiple languages.

In the last chapter, the dependency trees for our echo client and server were as follows:

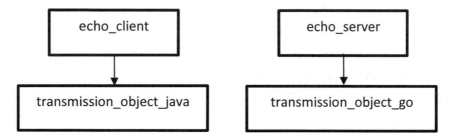

Figure 6-1. *Dependency trees for the JSON echo client and server*

As noted earlier, a major downfall is that the definitions for the JSON objects are specific to each language without reference to one another. Any change in the API (i.e., by changing the JSON object) needs to be done in both locations, making it prone to errors when you change it in one place and not the other.

Compare this to the dependency tree created for our Protocol Buffer echo client and server:

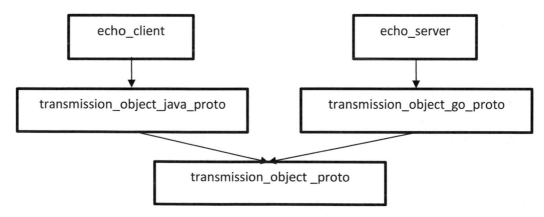

Figure 6-2. *Dependency tree for the Protocol Buffer echo client and server*

Now the dependency tree for the Protocol Buffer echo client and server is still relatively simple and likely familiar to anyone coding at scale. However, the remarkable aspects of it are the following: (a) we are tying together dependencies across three languages (i.e., Java, Go, Protocol Buffer); (b) by doing so, we are solving the API change management problem from the JSON client; and (c) we have done so using relatively little setup code.

Change Management in Action

Having set up our build dependency tree, now let's see it work in practice. First, we will ensure that all of our targets are already up to date.

Make sure that all of your targets are built using the special all target:

```
chapter_06/src$ bazel build :all
INFO: Analysed 5 targets (43 packages loaded, 7657 targets configured).
INFO: Found 5 targets...
INFO: Elapsed time: 12.039s, Critical Path: 1.03s
INFO: 0 processes.
INFO: Build completed successfully, 1 total action
```

Now let's check the timestamp on our build targets of echo_client and echo_server:

```
chapter_06/src$ ll ../bazel-bin/src/echo_client.jar
-r-xr-xr-x  1 pj   wheel   12168 Jun 18 22:06 ../bazel-bin/src/echo_client.jar

chapter_06/src$ ll ../bazel-bin/src/darwin_amd64_stripped/echo_server
-r-xr-xr-x  1 pj   wheel   3595880 Jun 18 23:14 ../bazel-bin/src/darwin_
amd64_stripped/echo_server
```

Make a trivial change to the echo_sever.go, but still ensure it still compiles (e.g., change some text in a log statement). Now let's rebuild everything again and recheck the timestamps:

```
chapter_06/src$ bazel build :all
INFO: Analysed 5 targets (1 packages loaded, 126 targets configured).
INFO: Found 5 targets...
INFO: Elapsed time: 1.103s, Critical Path: 0.55s
INFO: 2 processes: 2 darwin-sandbox.
INFO: Build completed successfully, 3 total actions
```

```
chapter_06/src$ ll ../bazel-bin/src/echo_client.jar
-r-xr-xr-x  1 pj  wheel  12168 Jun 18 22:06 ../bazel-bin/src/echo_client.jar
```

```
chapter_06/src$ ll ../bazel-bin/src/darwin_amd64_stripped/echo_server
-r-xr-xr-x  1 pj  wheel  3595880 Jun 20 03:10 ../bazel-bin/src/darwin_
amd64_stripped/echo_server
```

Unsurprisingly, Bazel only had to rebuild echo_server since our changes were confined only to that target.

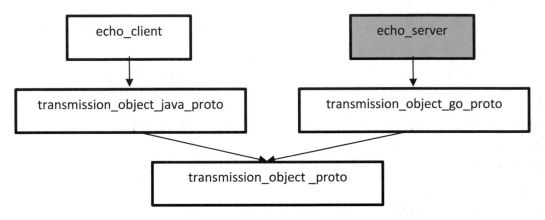

Figure 6-3. *Changes to the echo_server only affect a single target*

However, let's make a more substantial change; let's remove a field from the TransmissionObject message.

Listing 6-11. Removing the Message field from TransmissionObject

```
syntax = "proto3";

package transmission_object;

message TransmissionObject {
    float value = 1;
    // string message = 2;
}
```

Now, let's attempt to rebuild both echo_client and echo_server:

Note   You will notice that we add the flag keep_going (or a shortened version of -k) to the build command. Without this, the "build everything" command would stop at the first failure; using it, we see all targets that are failing.

```
chapter_06/src$ bazel build --keep_going :all
INFO: Analysed 5 targets (0 packages loaded, 0 targets configured).
INFO: Found 5 targets...
ERROR: chapter_06/src/BUILD:12:1: Couldn't build file src/echo_client.jar:
Building src/echo_
client.jar (1 source file) failed (Exit 1)
src/EchoClient.java:22: error: cannot find symbol
                    .setMessage(inputFromUser)
                    ^
  symbol:    method setMessage(String)
  location: class Builder
ERROR: chapter_06/src/BUILD:27:1: Couldn't build file src/darwin_amd64_
stripped/echo_server%/
src/echo_server.a: GoCompile src/darwin_amd64_stripped/echo_server%/src/
echo_server.a failed (Exit 1) builder failed: error executing command
bazel-out/host/bin/external/go_sdk/builder compile -sdk external/go_sdk
-installsuffix darwin_amd64 -src src/echo_server.go -arc ... (remaining 12
argument(s) skipped)

Use --sandbox_debug to see verbose messages from the sandbox
compile: error running compiler: exit status 2
/private/var/tmp/_bazel_pj/e24198bf4e647dabf052e612ba765c04/sandbox/darwin-
sandbox/1/execroot/__main__/src/echo_server.go:41:47: transmissionObject
.GetMessage undefined (type *transmission_object.TransmissionObject has no
field or method GetMessage)
/private/var/tmp/_bazel_pj/e24198bf4e647dabf052e612ba765c04/sandbox/darwin-
sandbox/1/execroot/__main__/src/echo_server.go:44:20: transmissionObject.
Message undefined (type *transmission_object.TransmissionObject has no
field or method Message)
```

```
/private/var/tmp/_bazel_pj/e24198bf4e647dabf052e612ba765c04/sandbox/darwin-
sandbox/1/execroot/__main__/src/echo_server.go:44:70: transmissionObject.
GetMessage undefined (type *transmission_object.TransmissionObject has no
field or method GetMessage)
INFO: Elapsed time: 0.364s, Critical Path: 0.18s
INFO: 0 processes.
FAILED: Build did NOT complete successfully
```

In this case, by changing the base dependency, we have dirtied our entire dependency tree:

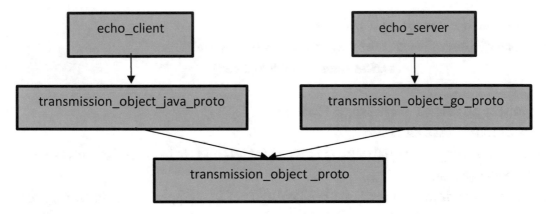

Figure 6-4. *Changes to the transmission_object_proto affect all targets*

If you'd like, you can double check the modification date after you fix the code by restoring the field.

Final Word

In this chapter, you were able to very simply add and use the necessary functionality for Protocol Buffers. Along the way, you also got to see firsthand the abilities of Bazel to very easily and powerfully manage build dependencies, even between code written in multiple languages. Although the examples here truly only scratched the surface, already you should be able to see the possibilities provided by a simple and standard declarative build language.

Protocol Buffers also reinforced Bazel's capabilities at handling multiple languages with ease. At the same time, you also got a glimpse into easily using Protocol Buffers for serialization across multiple languages.

In later chapters, we will be returning to more use of Protocol Buffers with Bazel. For the moment, however, we will take a step back and look at some facilities that Bazel provides for code organization.

CHAPTER 7

Code Organization and Bazel

Over the last several chapters, the examples kept all of the code in a single directory. While this was convenient for illustration purposes, this will not work in practice. Furthermore, the examples often broke from established directory and package patterns found (and even enforced) in certain languages (e.g., Java, Go, etc.). In this chapter, we will correct the organizational shortcomings of prior chapters and demonstrate the facilities Bazel provides for working within a hierarchical directory structure.

Note The directory structure we create here will be used throughout the rest of the book.

Setup

The majority of work we will do here reorganizes work from the prior chapter. For the most part, we will not be creating any new functionality. To accelerate our work, let's first copy over the last chapter's work into a new directory. Just before we do that, we will also clean up any builds from our prior chapter:

```
$ cd chapter_06
chapter_06$ bazel clean
chapter_06$ ls
WORKSPACE      src
```

© P.J. McNerney 2020
P.J. McNerney, *Beginning Bazel*, https://doi.org/10.1007/978-1-4842-5194-2_7

Having cleaned up any prior cached files, now let's copy over the last chapter's work:

```
chapter_06$ cd ..
$ cp -rf chapter_06 chapter_07
$ cd chapter_07
chapter_07 $ ls
WORKSPACE        src
```

If you would like, you can confirm that all is working as expected by executing a build or run command for a target from the last chapter. If you do, also fire off a `clean` command; though this is strictly not necessary, it will help with keeping your top-level directory for the reorganization task.

Separating the Protocol Buffers

There are many ways to reorganize your code (e.g., language, client vs. server, etc.); beyond Bazel's natural inclination toward a monorepo, however, this chapter does not offer any kind of strong opinion on this matter (i.e., do what makes sense for your project).

However, one obvious separation that we can do here is to pull out the files at build targets that encompass the various BUILD targets and definitions for the Protocol Buffers. These are referenced by both the client and the server *and* are their own language, so they can be easily pulled out from the current conglomerate directory.

First, let's create a top-level directory (`proto`) and move the Protocol Buffer definition from its current location:

```
chapter_07$ mkdir proto
chapter_07$ mv src/transmission_object.proto proto/
```

Next, we will create a new BUILD file, which will hold all of our protobuf build targets:

```
chapter_07$ cd proto/
chapter_07/proto$ touch BUILD
```

Listing 7-1. Protobuf-only BUILD file

```
load("@io_bazel_rules_go//proto:def.bzl", "go_proto_library")

proto_library(
    name = "transmission_object_proto",
```

```
    srcs = ["transmission_object.proto"],
)

java_proto_library(
    name = "transmission_object_java_proto",
    deps = [":transmission_object_proto"],
)

go_proto_library(
    name = "transmission_object_go_proto",
    proto = ":transmission_object_proto",
    importpath = "transmission_object"
)
```

Save this to proto/BUILD.

Now, remove the corresponding targets (e.g., src:transmission_object_proto and so on) from src/BUILD. This will temporarily render the other build targets within that BUILD file unbuildable, but this will be fixed shortly.

Finally, let's verify that our targets are building correctly within our new directory:

```
chapter_07/proto$ bazel build :all
INFO: Analysed 3 targets (23 packages loaded, 6994 targets configured).
INFO: Found 3 targets...
INFO: Elapsed time: 0.993s, Critical Path: 0.35s
INFO: 4 processes: 3 darwin-sandbox, 1 worker.
INFO: Build completed successfully, 5 total actions
```

Referencing Build Targets Outside of the Current Package

The previous examples had taken advantage of their colocation within the same directory/package to easily specify the dependencies among BUILD targets. Since everything was in the same location, each example's build targets could specify local build targets (or would refer to external dependencies).

In separating out our Protocol Buffer build targets into a separate package, we broke our existing targets. Attempting to build one of our existing targets will lead to failure:

```
chapter_07$ bazel build src:echo_client
ERROR: chapter_07/ src/BUILD:5:12: in deps attribute
        of java_binary rule //src:echo_client: target '//src:transmission_
        object_java_proto' does not exist
ERROR: Analysis of target '//src:echo_client' failed; build aborted:
        Analysis of target '//src:echo_client' failed; build aborted
INFO: Elapsed time: 0.117s
INFO: 0 processes.
FAILED: Build did NOT complete successfully (1 packages loaded, 2 targets
        configured)
```

Let's correct each of our BUILD targets so that we can correctly refer to the newly created, nonlocal Protocol Buffer dependencies. Open the src/BUILD file (changes in bold).

Listing 7-2. Updating the src/BUILD dependencies

```
java_binary(
    name = "echo_client",
    srcs = ["EchoClient.java"],
    main_class = "EchoClient",
    deps = ["//proto:transmission_object_java_proto"],
)

load("@io_bazel_rules_go//go:def.bzl", "go_binary")
go_binary(
    name = "echo_server",
    srcs = ["echo_server.go"],
    deps = [
        "//proto:transmission_object_go_proto",
        "@com_github_golang_protobuf//proto:go_default_library",
    ],
)
```

Save the changes to src/BUILD.

One feature of Bazel is that, beyond the allowance for local dependencies, all dependency references are absolute paths with respect to a particular WORKSPACE. For the preceding examples, when we specified the dependencies on the newly created protobuf targets, this was done with respect to the root of the WORKSPACE (which is indicated by //). This is an important point: dependencies are not specified using paths relative to the current BUILD file. Although this may seem like an onerous requirement, it stems from the general Bazel theme of making everything explicit.

As seen previously, we can also refer to dependencies that are pulled into the WORKSPACE (e.g., our Go rules) by using the @ symbol prior to the name of the dependency; this informs Bazel of a dependency that is nonlocal to the WORKSPACE.

However, despite having correctly referred to our newly created targets, we will run into one more problem. To illustrate, let's run our build one more time:

```
chapter_07$ bazel build src:echo_client
ERROR: /chapter_07/src/BUILD:1:1: in java_binary rule //src:echo_client:
        target '//proto:transmission_object_java_proto' is not visible from
        target '//src:echo_client'. Check the visibility declaration of the
        former target if you think the dependency is legitimate
ERROR: Analysis of target '//src:echo_client' failed; build aborted:
        Analysis of target '//src:echo_client' failed; build aborted
INFO: Elapsed time: 0.215s
INFO: 0 processes.
FAILED: Build did NOT complete successfully (6 packages loaded, 390 targets
        configured)
```

We will correct this problem within the next section.

Target Visibility

Many object-oriented languages (e.g., Java, C++, Objective-C, etc.) have a concept of *visibility* into an object's member variables and functions. Typically, this is framed in the concepts of *interface* (i.e., the public-facing API) and *implementation* (i.e., the code that is used to actually perform the work). This division is hammered in countless coding books to achieve a *separation of concerns*. In theory, this gives the implementation the ability to change without affecting clients of said functionality; they all conform to the same interface.

In many languages, visibility need not be a binary choice; it is possible to specify visibility to some particular characteristic (e.g., members only visible to subclasses of a parent class, members only visible to the same Java package, etc.). This provides flexibility in terms of what pieces should be visible and to whom.

Bazel contains a powerful mechanism for target visibility, enabling the architect of the project to determine what should be visible and to whom. Notably, this is a *language-agnostic* feature; any build target can take advantage of this particular Bazel feature, regardless of whether the language itself implements a form of member visibility. This enables us to determine which portions of our code should be considered valid for "public" consumption (i.e., the *interface*) and which should be retained privately (i.e., the *implementation*).

Throughout the course of this book, we have ignored the notion of visibility. This was enabled by virtue of all our code existing within the same directory and BUILD file (i.e., within the same Bazel package); all targets within a given package are automatically visible to one another. Additionally, without any additional specification, all targets within a given package are, by default, *invisible* to any external targets. That is, unless we actually make an explicit declaration regarding its visibility, a given target *cannot be depended upon outside of its own package.*

Although this might seem like an onerous requirement, it is actually one of the most powerful aspects of Bazel: as the author of your own code, you get to decide how best to structure it for building *and* how best to structure it for clients to use. These two need not be the same thing.

Since we *do* want clients external to a given package to make use of our code, we will need to specify the visibility. There are two major ways to accomplish this: (1) the package level and (2) the target level. We will explore both ways.

Package Visibility

As mentioned earlier, the default is that all targets within a given package are unavailable as dependencies by other targets which are external to the package. The simplest approach we can take is to make *all* targets visible.

Open the proto/BUILD file and add the following directive.

Listing 7-3. Making all build targets visible

```
package(default_visibility = ["//visibility:public"])

load("@io_bazel_rules_go//proto:def.bzl", "go_proto_library")
```

```
proto_library(
    name = "transmission_object_proto",
    srcs = ["transmission_object.proto"],
)

java_proto_library(
    name = "transmission_object_java_proto",
    deps = [":transmission_object_proto"],
)

go_proto_library(
    name = "transmission_object_go_proto",
    proto = ":transmission_object_proto",
    importpath = "transmission_object"
)
```

Save to proto/BUILD.

Now, let's attempt to build src:echo_client again:

```
chapter_07$ bazel build src:echo_client
INFO: Analysed target //src:echo_client (1 packages loaded, 4 targets
      configured).
INFO: Found 1 target...
Target //src:echo_client up-to-date:
  bazel-bin/src/echo_client.jar
  bazel-bin/src/echo_client
INFO: Elapsed time: 3.221s, Critical Path: 2.83s
INFO: 2 processes: 1 darwin-sandbox, 1 worker.
INFO: Build completed successfully, 6 total actions
```

Now that we have updated the visibility of the dependencies, our build works as expected (src:echo_server should also work, but that is left as an exercise to the reader).

Note   Once again, an astute reader will note that we have include yet-another-new function(package) into our *BUILD* file. The package function exists to apply the same metadata to all targets within a given package. In this case, we are only using it to make modifications to the visibility.

Path-Specific Visibility

The prior section's solution solved the immediate problem of getting the echo_client and echo_server targets to build. However, the solution of making *every* target within the package visible is heavy-handed to say the least. This kind of "all-or-nothing" approach doesn't really lend itself to good code organization; in the limit it is only slightly better than putting everything into the same place.

Fortunately, we can do better. Bazel provides the ability to explicitly specify paths for target visibility. In this case, let's restrict access to only the *src* package.

Open the proto/BUILD file, and let's modify our visibility specification.

Listing 7-4. Restricting the visibility to a specific package

```
package(default_visibility = ["//src:__pkg__"])

load("@io_bazel_rules_go//proto:def.bzl", "go_proto_library")
<omitted for brevity>
```

Save the proto/BUILD file.

Reconfirm that you are able to build both src:echo_client and src:echo_server. Now you have reduced the visibility to *only* targets that are strictly within the src package.

Note   Although the //src:__pkg__ specification will allow access to any proto target from within the src package, this specification does **not** automatically include any *subpackages* of src. That is, if you had a package such as //src/client, then the *proto* targets would **not** be visible to the targets within //src/client.

This can easily be addressed by modifying the visibility specification from __pkg__ to __subpackages__. This indicates that a given dependency should be visible both to a particular package and any subpackages therein.

Individual Target Visibility

In the last section, we specified the visibility at the package level. While this is always a good starting point, it still echoes the earlier "all-or-nothing" problem; we are still making statements about the visibility across all of the targets within a given package. Yet again, Bazel comes to the rescue.

Individual targets can declare their visibility; that is, each individual target can specify what other packages may depend upon it. This includes having an individual target make the blanket statement of visibility:public.

Open the proto/BUILD file; we are going to make some modifications to the individual target visibilities.

Listing 7-5. Specifying visibility at the build target level

```
#package(default_visibility = ["//src: :__pkg__"])

load("@io_bazel_rules_go//proto:def.bzl", "go_proto_library")

proto_library(
    name = "transmission_object_proto",
    srcs = ["transmission_object.proto"],
)

java_proto_library(
    name = "transmission_object_java_proto",
    deps = [":transmission_object_proto"],
    visibility = ["//src:__pkg__"],
)

go_proto_library(
    name = "transmission_object_go_proto",
    proto = ":transmission_object_proto",
    importpath = "transmission_object",
)
```

Save proto/BUILD. Now, let's verify once again that our src:echo_client still builds:

```
chapter_07$ bazel build src:echo_client
INFO: Analysed target //src:echo_client (1 packages loaded, 4 targets
    configured).
```

```
INFO: Found 1 target...
Target //src:echo_client up-to-date:
  bazel-bin/src/echo_client.jar
  bazel-bin/src/echo_client
INFO: Elapsed time: 0.207s, Critical Path: 0.00s
INFO: 0 processes.
INFO: Build completed successfully, 1 total action
```

However, you will get a different result when trying to build *src:echo_server*:

```
chapter_07$ bazel build src:echo_server
ERROR: chapter_07/src/BUILD:10:1: in go_binary rule //src:echo_server:
       target '//proto:transmission_object_go_proto' is not visible from
       target '//src:echo_server'. Check the visibility declaration of the
       former target if you think the dependency is legitimate
ERROR: Analysis of target '//src:echo_server' failed; build aborted:
       Analysis of target '//src:echo_server' failed; build aborted
INFO: Elapsed time: 0.109s
INFO: 0 processes.
FAILED: Build did NOT complete successfully (0 packages loaded, 1 target
       configured)
```

Here, we removed the package level directive to make every target visible to all of *src*. Instead, we only made the *transmission_object_java_proto* target (required only by *echo_client*) visible to the *src* package. The *transmission_object_go_proto* (required by *echo_server*) is once again invisible.

Obviously, we can easily fix this. Reopen the *proto/BUILD* file and add the visibility specification to *transmission_object_go_proto*.

Listing 7-6. Fixing the visibility for transmission_object_go_proto

```
#package(default_visibility = ["//src:echo_client"])

load("@io_bazel_rules_go//proto:def.bzl", "go_proto_library")

proto_library(
    name = "transmission_object_proto",
    srcs = ["transmission_object.proto"],
)
```

```
java_proto_library(
    name = "transmission_object_java_proto",
    deps = [":transmission_object_proto"],
    visibility = ["//src:__pkg__"],
)

go_proto_library(
    name = "transmission_object_go_proto",
    proto = ":transmission_object_proto",
    importpath = "transmission_object",
    visibility = ["//src:__pkg__"],
)
```

Save the file to *proto/BUILD* and retry building *src:echo_server*:

```
chapter_07$ bazel build src:echo_server
INFO: Analysed target //src:echo_server (1 packages loaded, 4 targets
     configured).
INFO: Found 1 target...
Target //src:echo_server up-to-date:
  bazel-bin/src/darwin_amd64_stripped/echo_server
INFO: Elapsed time: 0.227s, Critical Path: 0.01s
INFO: 0 processes.
INFO: Build completed successfully, 1 total action
```

Having fixed the dependency visibility, all builds are now happy again.

Mixing Package and Target Visibilities

Having demonstrated two different ways (i.e., both *package* and *individual* targets) to express visibility, it is important to also mention how they interact with each other.

Simply put, package level visibility specifications act as a *default value* for all targets within a package. Individual visibility specifications act as the *final* value for the visibility of that particular target. That is, there is no attempt to merge the values between the package and individual specifications; it is always a replacement operation.

Although this might seem draconian, an important thing to remember is that Bazel seeks to make things explicit; complicated implicit merging among visibility rules does not serve this purpose. Yes, this might entail some extra typing when trying to create some very particular rules; however, being explicit wins out over momentary convenience.

Bazel provides a mitigating strategy to this verbosity through the construct of a package_group. A package_group allows you to assign metadata (e.g., visibility rules) across a set of packages. This provides a nice middle ground between assigning visibility to individual targets and requiring a package-wide visibility policy.

Separating the Client and Server Code

Having separated our protobuf code into its own package, we will also separate out the client and server code into their own packages.

Separating the Echo Server Code

Let's first create a directory for the echo_server. For reasons that will become more obvious later on (and in later chapters), we'll create a sub-directory for the echo_server and move the corresponding code into that directory:

```
chapter_07$ mkdir -p server/echo_server
chapter_07$ mv src/echo_server.go server/echo_server/echo_server.go
```

Now let's create a server/echo_server/BUILD file. We will just copy the prior definition for the echo_server build target in the original src/BUILD file.

Listing 7-7. Creating the server/echo_server/BUILD file

```
load("@io_bazel_rules_go//go:def.bzl", "go_binary")
go_binary(
    name = "echo_server",
    srcs = ["echo_server.go"],
    deps = [
        "//proto:transmission_object_go_proto",
        "@com_github_golang_protobuf//proto:go_default_library",
    ],
)
```

Save that file to server/echo_server/BUILD. Trying to build this will simply reintroduce the proto visibility issues we saw earlier. Let's first update the visibility rules for the necessary target.

Open the proto/BUILD file and make the following modifications.

Listing 7-8. Updating the visibility package for transmission_object_go_proto

```
load("@io_bazel_rules_go//proto:def.bzl", "go_proto_library")

proto_library(
    name = "transmission_object_proto",
    srcs = ["transmission_object.proto"],
)

java_proto_library(
    name = "transmission_object_java_proto",
    deps = [":transmission_object_proto"],
    visibility = ["//src:__pkg__"],
)

go_proto_library(
    name = "transmission_object_go_proto",
    proto = ":transmission_object_proto",
    importpath = "transmission_object",
    visibility = ["//server/echo_server:__pkg__"],
)
```

Save the changes to proto/BUILD. Now, we should be able to successfully build our newly minted server/echo_server:echo_server target:

```
chapter_07$ bazel build server/echo_server:echo_server
INFO: Analysed target //server/echo_server:echo_server (2 packages loaded,
    5 targets configured).
INFO: Found 1 target...
Target //server/echo_server:echo_server up-to-date:
  bazel-bin/server/echo_server/darwin_amd64_stripped/echo_server
INFO: Elapsed time: 0.896s, Critical Path: 0.56s
INFO: 2 processes: 2 darwin-sandbox.
INFO: Build completed successfully, 5 total actions
```

Eliding the Build Target

One thing to note is that we have a duplication in the path to build the echo_server; specifically, we see "echo_server" twice:

```
chapter_07$ bazel build server/echo_server:echo_server
```

One allowance that Bazel provides is eliding the build target when it is the same name as its containing package. That is, the following invocation is functionally equivalent:

```
chapter_07$ bazel build server/echo_server
INFO: Analysed target //server/echo_server:echo_server (1 packages loaded,
    2 targets configured).
INFO: Found 1 target...
Target //server/echo_server:echo_server up-to-date:
  bazel-bin/server/echo_server/darwin_amd64_stripped/echo_server
INFO: Elapsed time: 0.217s, Critical Path: 0.00s
INFO: 0 processes.
INFO: Build completed successfully, 1 total action
```

While it might be tempting to cry foul at this point in time for Bazel, this convenience is providing a very powerful convention: if a target has an identical name to the package wherein it is contained, then it can be considered the "public"-facing target (i.e., the *interface*) for that package. This normalizes and simplifies expectations from external packages about which target(s) one should depend upon.

Notably, this convention is not a *requirement* of Bazel, but its existence is extremely powerful and can help reduce cognitive load when creating and analyzing build dependency trees.

Separating the Echo Client Code

Having taken care of the server side of the equation, we finally turn our attention to the client as well. In this case, we will create a very slightly different directory/package structure; this is in anticipation of later chapters. As before, we will move the appropriate code into the sub-directory:

```
chapter_07$ mkdir -p client/echo_client/command_line
chapter_07$ mv src/EchoClient.java client/echo_client/command_line/
EchoClient.java
```

Now we need to create the appropriate BUILD file; once again, we will end up just copying out the previous definition of the target.

Listing 7-9. Creating the client/echo_client/command_line/BUILD file

```
java_binary(
    name = "command_line",
    srcs = ["EchoClient.java"],
    main_class = "EchoClient",
    deps = ["//proto:transmission_object_java_proto"],
)
```

Save the changes down to the client/echo_client/command_line/BUILD file. Once again, we will need to update the appropriate proto/BUILD target visibility; otherwise, our echo_client target will once again fail to build.

Open proto/BUILD and make the following changes to the transmission_object_java_proto.

Listing 7-10. Updating the visibility for transmission_object_java_proto

```
load("@io_bazel_rules_go//proto:def.bzl", "go_proto_library")

proto_library(
    name = "transmission_object_proto",
    srcs = ["transmission_object.proto"],
)

java_proto_library(
    name = "transmission_object_java_proto",
    deps = [":transmission_object_proto"],
    visibility = ["//client/echo_client:__subpackages__"],
)

go_proto_library(
    name = "transmission_object_go_proto",
    proto = ":transmission_object_proto",
    importpath = "transmission_object",
    visibility = ["//server/echo_server:__pkg__"],
)
```

Save the file to `proto/BUILD`.

Note   You might notice that we have created a slightly different specification for the visibility for `transmission_object_java_proto` vs. its Go counterpart. In particular, while the Go version was very specifically targeted toward the `echo_server` package, the Java version has a wider set of potential packages (i.e., everything under the `echo_client` package). This is again done in anticipation of upcoming chapters.

Having updated the visibility, let's verify that our target still builds as expected (taking advantage of the aforementioned target elision):

```
chapter_07$ bazel build client/echo_client/command_line
INFO: Analysed target //client/echo_client/command_line:command_line
      (1 packages loaded, 2 targets configured).
INFO: Found 1 target...
Target //client/echo_client/command_line:command_line up-to-date:
  bazel-bin/client/echo_client/command_line/command_line.jar
  bazel-bin/client/echo_client/command_line/command_line
INFO: Elapsed time: 0.192s, Critical Path: 0.01s
INFO: 0 processes.
INFO: Build completed successfully, 1 total action
```

Cleaning Up

Having stripped the original directory of basically everything, we can now get rid of it:

```
chapter_07$ rm -rf src
```

Just as a sanity check, we can reconfirm that everything builds as expected through a blanket build command:

```
chapter_07$ bazel build ...
INFO: Analysed 5 targets (0 packages loaded, 0 targets configured).
INFO: Found 5 targets...
```

```
INFO: Elapsed time: 0.188s, Critical Path: 0.01s
INFO: 0 processes.
INFO: Build completed successfully, 1 total action
```

Since we did not change any actual code, just move it around and create/reconfigure BUILD files and targets; all functionality should work as before. Verification is left as an exercise to the reader.

Final Word

Over the course of the last chapter, you employed the tools of Bazel to reorganize the code into a (more) scalable development structure. Although still toy examples, there should be enough content to begin to use the constructs of Bazel to craft your code structure into something easy to understand, scalable, and controllable.

Although what was done within this chapter represents one particular organization, it should not be considered canonical by any means. For example, the location and visibility of the Protocol Buffer and derived language-specific targets may be changed (e.g., bring the language-specific proto targets closer to their actually usage). Another example would be changing to a language-centric directory/package structure.

There is no "right" answer; there are trade-offs to each possibility. Regardless, Bazel flexibly supports the type of code organization that best suits your needs while providing tools that aid in maintaining this structure over time.

CHAPTER 8

gRPC and Bazel

In Chapter 6, you discovered the use of Protocol Buffers to provide a succinct, well-typed, and easily serialized data description that worked across languages. As a corollary, Bazel provided an easy way to depend upon the Protocol Buffers. In this chapter, we will explore the use of Protocol Buffers to also easily define APIs to work across various languages.

The Protocol Buffer format is used to define APIs via gRPC, which is Google's way of creating *remote procedure calls* (RPCs). In a similar fashion to Protocol Buffers normalizing data access across multiple languages, gRPC normalizes making RPCs from clients to servers.

Setup

We will build off of everything done in the last chapter. We will start by first copying everything from the last chapter into a new directory (after verifying that we have cleaned out all build products):

```
$ cd chapter_07
chapter_07$ bazel clean
chapter_07$ ls
WORKSPACE    client    proto    server

chapter_07$ cd ..
$ cp -rf chapter_07 chapter_08
$ cd chapter_08
chapter_08$
```

Finally, we need to add more dependencies within the WORKSPACE file. Add in the highlighted changes into your WORKSPACE file.

© P.J. McNerney 2020
P.J. McNerney, *Beginning Bazel*, https://doi.org/10.1007/978-1-4842-5194-2_8

Listing 8-1. Adding the gRPC dependencies to the WORKSPACE

```
load("@bazel_tools//tools/build_defs/repo:http.bzl", "http_archive")

skylib_version = "0.8.0"

http_archive(
    name = "bazel_skylib",
    url = "https://github.com/bazelbuild/bazel-skylib/releases/download/{}/
    bazel-skylib.{}.tar.gz".format(skylib_version, skylib_version),
)

<existing dependencies omitted for brevity>
http_archive(
    name = "io_grpc_grpc_java",
    strip_prefix = "grpc-java-1.24.0",
    urls = ["https://github.com/grpc/grpc-java/archive/v1.24.0.tar.gz"],
)
load("@io_grpc_grpc_java//:repositories.bzl", "grpc_java_repositories")
grpc_java_repositories()

http_archive(
    name = "bazel_gazelle",
    urls = ["https://github.com/bazelbuild/bazel-gazelle/releases/download/
    v0.19.1/bazel-gazelle-v0.19.1.tar.gz"],
)
load("@bazel_gazelle//:deps.bzl", "gazelle_dependencies", "go_repository")
gazelle_dependencies()

go_repository(
    name = "org_golang_google_grpc",
    build_file_proto_mode = "disable",
    importpath = "google.golang.org/grpc",
    sum = "h1:J0UbZOIrCAl+fpTOf8YLs4dJo8L/owV4LYVtAXQoPkw=",
    version = "v1.22.0",
)
```

```
go_repository(
    name = "org_golang_x_net",
    importpath = "golang.org/x/net",
    sum = "h1:oWX7TPOiFAMXLq8ooikBYfCJVlRHBcsciT5bXOrH628=",
    version = "v0.0.0-20190311183353-d8887717615a",
)

go_repository(
    name = "org_golang_x_text",
    importpath = "golang.org/x/text",
    sum = "h1:g61tztE5qeGQ89tm6NTjjM9VPImo88od1l6aSorWRWg=",
    version = "v0.3.0",
)
```

Save to the WORKSPACE file.

As one final item, we are going to create an empty BUILD file right next to our WORKSPACE file. This is related to the use of Gazelle (discussed next).

```
chapter_08$ touch BUILD
```

Dependency Discussion

It is worthwhile to take a moment and discuss some of the dependencies that we just added, particularly for Go. The use of http_archive should be rote by this point in time.

Skylib

The Skylib library contains a number of useful functions and rules that are used when creating custom build rules. It is a common dependency that is used by many packages. As such, you can run into issues when dependencies use multiple versions of this library. In this case, we are adding in this library explicitly and asserting a version that will be used throughout your WORKSPACE.

One thing to note about *how* we are including this particular version of Skylib. If you notice, we are using the .format() function on the string in order to insert the version into the path. This allows us to easily change the version later on. It also demonstrates the use of Python-like features of Starlark to create richer specification of our dependencies.

Gazelle

Gazelle is unique in that it is a build file generator for Bazel projects. That is, it can auto-magically generate BUILD files for a language from code (assuming, of course, that the code is well formed). Gazelle supports Go out-of-the-box. Since Go has the very nice property of being able to very explicitly specify dependencies within the code itself, Gazelle is able to take advantage of this fact and generate BUILD files for you.

Gazelle also defines a repository rule for Go, aptly named go_repository. As you might have already guessed, go_repository allows you to (a) specify an import path from which to retrieve the necessary dependency and (b) auto-generate the necessary BUILD files for the packages therein. As you can imagine, this can be of enormous help when incorporating third party libraries (at least for Go) that do not already have Bazel support.

The BUILD file at the root of your project functions as a location to configure options for Gazelle, if you want to use its functionality in your own project. If the BUILD file is missing, your project will fail to build.

Defining the gRPC in Protocol Buffers

In a similar fashion to how we defined messages in Protocol Buffers in a language-agnostic way, we can also define interfaces for RPCs. We will create a new file within the proto directory to house the new API.

Listing 8-2. Defining the interface for the RPC

```
syntax = "proto3";

import "proto/transmission_object.proto";

package transceiver;

message EchoRequest {
    transmission_object.TransmissionObject from_client = 1;
}

message EchoResponse {
    transmission_object.TransmissionObject from_server = 1;
}
```

```
service Transceiver {
    rpc Echo (EchoRequest) returns (EchoResponse);
}
```

Save this to proto/transceiver.proto.

Let's take a moment just to analyze these definitions. We locally define two messages EchoRequest and EchoResponse to contain the request and response to the RPC, respectively.

Notably, within both EchoRequest and EchoResponse, we include the earlier created TransmissionObject message. Strictly speaking, there is nothing required in having the same message being included in both the request and the response; we do this here only to mirror the functionality that we have created in prior chapters. Additionally, nothing requires having the messages for the request and response defined within the same file as the interface; we do so here only for the sake of simplicity.

We then define a service Transceiver, within which we have a single RPC, *Echo*. In the definition of Echo, we defined the required request and response.

Finally note that all we are doing here is defining the interface for our RPC. Beyond that, nothing (here) defines its implementation.

In order to actually use and generate the RPC, we need to update our proto/BUILD file with the appropriate build targets. Open the proto/BUILD file and add the following.

Listing 8-3. Defining the build targets for the Transceiver service

```
<omitted for brevity>
proto_library(
    name = "transceiver_proto",
    srcs = ["transceiver.proto"],
    deps = [
        ":transmission_object_proto",
    ]
)

go_proto_library(
    name = "transceiver_go_proto_grpc",
    compiler = "@io_bazel_rules_go//proto:go_grpc",
    proto = ":transceiver_proto",
    importpath = "transceiver",
```

```
    deps = [":transmission_object_go_proto",],
    visibility = ["//server/echo_server:__pkg__"],
)

java_proto_library(
    name = "transceiver_java_proto",
    deps = [":transceiver_proto"],
    visibility = ["//client/echo_client:__subpackages__"],
)

load("@io_grpc_grpc_java//:java_grpc_library.bzl", "java_grpc_library")
java_grpc_library(
    name = "transceiver_java_proto_grpc",
    srcs = [":transceiver_proto"],
    deps = [":transceiver_java_proto"],
    visibility = ["//client/echo_client:__subpackages__"],
)
```

Save the file to proto/BUILD.

As with the proto code, let's examine what we've added here. The first new build target should look familiar; it simply defines the proto_library target for the transceiver.proto file. In a similar fashion, transceiver_java_proto should also look very familiar, as it defines the build target for the Java version of transceiver.proto.

The transceiver_go_proto_grpc looks very similar to what we have seen previously; the primary exception is addition of the *compiler* directive within go_proto_library target. This defines the rule that should be used when compiling the target in order to support gRPC. We use the standard rule found within the @io_bazel_rules_go dependency.

Since we are using Go only on the server side, we set the visibility to only the server subpackages.

The java_grpc_library does a similar job, except for defining the necessary target for Java. In a complementary fashion, we set the visibility to only the client subpackages.

Just to confirm that all is working well, let's build all the targets within the package:

```
chapter_08$ bazel build proto:all
INFO: Analysed 7 targets (0 packages loaded, 0 targets configured).
INFO: Found 7 targets...
```

```
INFO: Elapsed time: 0.316s, Critical Path: 0.07s
INFO: 3 processes: 3 darwin-sandbox.
INFO: Build completed successfully, 4 total actions
```

Upgrading the Client to Use gRPC

Having defined the gRPC interface, we will now upgrade the client to use it. For the most part, the code will look very similar to what we had done previously. We will highlight a few of the changes that are needed for the basic version.

We had previously created a Java client that explicitly transmitted a serialized object. We will make some modifications to the support using gRPC.

Open client/echo_client/command_line/EchoClient.java.

Listing 8-4. Using gRPC on the client side

```java
import io.grpc.ManagedChannel;
import io.grpc.ManagedChannelBuilder;
import java.io.BufferedReader;
import java.io.InputStreamReader;

import transmission_object.TransmissionObjectOuterClass.TransmissionObject;
import transceiver.TransceiverOuterClass.EchoRequest;
import transceiver.TransceiverOuterClass.EchoResponse;
import transceiver.TransceiverGrpc;

public class EchoClient {
    public static void main(String args[]) {
        System.out.println("Spinning up the Echo Client in Java...");
        try {
            final BufferedReader commandLineInput = new BufferedReader(new
            InputStreamReader(System.in));
            System.out.println("Waiting on input from the user...");
            final String inputFromUser = commandLineInput.readLine();
            if (inputFromUser != null) {
                ManagedChannel channel =
                    ManagedChannelBuilder
                      .forAddress("localhost", 1234)
```

```
                    .usePlaintext()
                    .build();
                TransceiverGrpc.TransceiverBlockingStub stub =
                    TransceiverGrpc.newBlockingStub(channel);
                EchoRequest request =  EchoRequest.newBuilder()
                    .setFromClient(
                        TransmissionObject.newBuilder()
                            .setMessage(inputFromUser)
                            .setValue(3.145f)
                            .build())
                    .build();
                EchoResponse response = stub.echo(request);
                System.out.println("Received Message from server: ");
                System.out.println(response);
                channel.shutdownNow();
            }
        } catch (Exception e) {
            System.err.println("Error: " + e);
        }
    }
}
```

Save the file to client/echo_client/command_line/EchoClient.java.

Taking another moment to examine the changes, we first create a ManagedChannel to open a channel on a specific port. This is then used to create a stub (TransceiverBlockingStub) for actually making the RPC. For the sake of simplicity, we use the most basic of stubs, which makes blocking calls for all of the service's RPCs (other, more flexible versions of the stub are possible, but are outside of the scope of this book).

The stub provides local methods which forward the calls through the channel. Once created, the stub makes it as easy to call an RPC as it would be a local method. The request is formulated and then used to call into the method, with the expected response.

To complete the functionality, let's upgrade the target in the client/echo_client/command_line/BUILD file. As before, much of the original target remains the same, so we can highlight the necessary changes.

Listing 8-5. Modifications for EchoClient to support gRPC

```
java_binary(
    name = "command_line",
    srcs = ["EchoClient.java"],
    main_class = "EchoClient",
    runtime_deps = [
        "@io_grpc_grpc_java//netty",
    ],
    deps = [
        "//proto:transmission_object_java_proto",
        "//proto:transceiver_java_proto",
        "//proto:transceiver_java_proto_grpc",
        "@io_grpc_grpc_java//api",
    ]
)
```

Save the file to *client/echo_client/command_line/BUILD*.

For what might be obvious at this point in time, we've added the new dependencies from the *proto* subpackage. Additionally, we've added both a typical static dependency (@io_grpc_grpc_java//api) as well as a new runtime dependency (@io_grpc_grpc_java//netty).

In this latter case, we specify that this is a runtime dependency since it is not explicitly requested in the code. If you attempted to remove *runtime_deps*, you would find that building the program would work perfectly fine. However, attempting to run the program would result in an error message requesting the runtime dependency.

We will build the target just to confirm that all is well:

```
chapter_08$ bazel build client/echo_client/command_line
INFO: Analysed target //client/echo_client/command_line:command_line (32
      packages loaded, 317 targets configured).
INFO: Found 1 target...
Target //client/echo_client/command_line:command_line up-to-date:
  bazel-bin/client/echo_client/command_line/command_line.jar
  bazel-bin/client/echo_client/command_line/command_line
```

```
INFO: Elapsed time: 6.648s, Critical Path: 6.14s
INFO: 21 processes: 18 darwin-sandbox, 3 worker.
INFO: Build completed successfully, 25 total actions
```

Notably, we won't be able to actually run the client yet; although we've successfully created a client that uses gRPC, we still need a service that implements the RPC.

Upgrading the Server to Use gRPC

To upgrade our server to use gRPC, we will need to register and fill in the functionality for the RPCs. gRPC generates most of the scaffolding for us; we just need to register our server and provide the appropriate methods to fulfill the contract.

As with the prior section, we can make some modifications on our existing code. Notably, in this case, we will be making more extensive modifications in order to support gRPC.

Open server/echo_server/echo_server.go and make the highlighted modifications.

Listing 8-6. Implementing the gRPC interface on the server side

```go
package main

import (
        "fmt"
        "log"
        "net"
        "transceiver"
        "transmission_object"

        "golang.org/x/net/context"
        "google.golang.org/grpc"
)

type EchoServer struct{}

func (es *EchoServer) Echo(context context.Context, request *transceiver.
EchoRequest) (*transceiver.EchoResponse, error) {
        log.Println("Message = " + (*request).FromClient.GetMessage())
        log.Println("Value = " +
            fmt.Sprintf("%f", (*request).FromClient.GetValue()))
```

```go
        server_message := "Received from client: " +
            (*request).FromClient.GetMessage()
        server_value := (*request).FromClient.Value * 2
        from_server := transmission_object.TransmissionObject{
                Message: server_message,
                Value:   server_value,
        }
        return &transceiver.EchoResponse{
                FromServer: &from_server,
        }, nil
}

func main() {
        log.Println("Spinning up the Echo Server in Go...")
        listen, error := net.Listen("tcp", ":1234")
        if error != nil {
                log.Panicln("Unable to listen: " + error.Error())
        }
        defer listen.Close()
        defer log.Println("Connection now closed.")

        grpc_server := grpc.NewServer()
        transceiver.RegisterTransceiverServer(grpc_server, &EchoServer{})

        error = grpc_server.Serve(listen)
        if error != nil {
                log.Panicln("Unable to start serving! Error: " + error.Error())
        }
}
```

Save the changes to server/echo_server/echo_server.go.

Once again, let's take a step back to examine the major changes. In this case, you've created a Go struct EchoServer which has a specially named method Echo.

The Echo method takes in a Context object and the EchoRequest that we had defined in the protobuf definition and returns the EchoResponse object. This method fulfills the contract required by the interface definition. In terms of functionality, although the body differs slightly from the prior version, you should be able to recognize the same functionality.

Within the body of main, we created a new server and registered our EchoServer. Having completed the setup, we then just start listening to incoming messages.

Now let's finish upgrading the target in the BUILD file to support this new functionality. Open server/echo_server/BUILD and make the following highlighted modifications.

Listing 8-7. Modification for echo_server to support gRPC

```
load("@io_bazel_rules_go//go:def.bzl", "go_binary")
go_binary(
    name = "echo_server",
    srcs = ["echo_server.go"],
    deps = [
        "//proto:transceiver_go_proto_grpc",
        "//proto:transmission_object_go_proto",
        "@org_golang_x_net//context:go_default_library",
        "@org_golang_google_grpc//:go_default_library",
    ]
)
```

Save your changes to server/echo_server/BUILD.

As before, the new org_golang_* dependencies are not invented from thin air; they've come from the Go dependency that we had defined within the WORKSPACE file.

Now, let's just do a sanity check on the build to make sure that it is all working as expected:

```
chapter_08$ bazel build server/echo_server
INFO: Analysed target //server/echo_server:echo_server (0 packages loaded,
    0 targets configured).
INFO: Found 1 target...
Target //server/echo_server:echo_server up-to-date:
  bazel-bin/server/echo_server/darwin_amd64_stripped/echo_server
INFO: Elapsed time: 0.227s, Critical Path: 0.00s
INFO: 0 processes.
INFO: Build completed successfully, 1 total action
```

Running the Client and the Server

Having completed both the client and the server, we are ready to actually use our new functionality.

Open a new terminal window. We will first start running the server.

```
chapter_08$ bazel run server/echo_server
INFO: Analysed target //server/echo_server:echo_server (83 packages loaded,
      7969 targets configured).
INFO: Found 1 target...
Target //server/echo_server:echo_server up-to-date:
  bazel-bin/server/echo_server/darwin_amd64_stripped/echo_server
INFO: Elapsed time: 110.524s, Critical Path: 27.33s
INFO: 466 processes: 466 darwin-sandbox.
INFO: Build completed successfully, 467 total actions
INFO: Build completed successfully, 467 total actions
2019/07/23 05:11:30 Spinning up the Echo Server in Go...
```

Having gotten the server listening, let's run the client to fire a response. Open a second terminal window and run the following, adding some input at the end:

```
chapter_08$ bazel run client/echo_client/command_line
INFO: Analysed target //client/echo_client/command_line:command_line
      (60 packages loaded, 919 targets configured).
INFO: Found 1 target...
Target //client/echo_client/command_line:command_line up-to-date:
  bazel-bin/client/echo_client/command_line/command_line.jar
  bazel-bin/client/echo_client/command_line/command_line
INFO: Elapsed time: 5.728s, Critical Path: 5.33s
INFO: 3 processes: 2 darwin-sandbox, 1 worker.
INFO: Build completed successfully, 4 total actions
INFO: Build completed successfully, 4 total actions
Spinning up the Echo Client in Java...
Waiting on input from the user...
This is a test using gRPC.
Received Message from server:
from_server {
```

```
  value: 6.29
  message: "Received from client: This is a test using gRPC."
}
```

We've successfully done the echo functionality using gRPC. However, let's take a look back at the server terminal to see the messages there:

```
chapter_08$ bazel run server/echo_server
<omitted for brevity>
INFO: Build completed successfully, 1 total action
2019/07/23 05:11:49 Spinning up the Echo Server in Go...
2019/07/23 05:15:02 Message = This is a test using gRPC.
2019/07/23 05:15:02 Value = 3.145000
```

As with your prior implementation, you see the message that was sent by the client. However, there is one important difference to the functionality here: the server has not exited. That is, the server is still running and waiting for new connections to come in.

To verify, switch back to your client terminal and do one more run:

```
chapter_08$ bazel run client/echo_client/command_line
<omitted for brevity>
Spinning up the Echo Client in Java...
Waiting on input from the user...
Still up and running
Received Message from server:
from_server {
  value: 6.29
  message: "Received from client: Still up and running"
}
```

Now let's look back on the server terminal to see the messages:

```
chapter_08$ bazel run server/echo_server
<omitted for brevity>
2019/07/23 05:11:49 Spinning up the Echo Server in Go...
2019/07/23 05:15:02 Message = This is a test using gRPC.
2019/07/23 05:15:02 Value = 3.145000
2019/07/23 05:21:20 Message = Still up and running
2019/07/23 05:21:20 Value = 3.145000
```

This persistent functionality is available "out of the box" with gRPC. In switching over to it, we've actually gained more functionality for roughly the same number of lines of code.

Adding Another RPC

One complaint which could arise is that you have written roughly the same amount of code to perform the same actions as before. To further illustrate the power of what we have created, we will quickly add one more RPC to the entire system.

Open proto/transceiver.proto and add the following highlighted lines.

Listing 8-8. Adding the interface for another RPC

```
syntax = "proto3";

import "proto/transmission_object.proto";

package transceiver;

message EchoRequest {
    transmission_object.TransmissionObject from_client = 1;
}
message EchoResponse {
    transmission_object.TransmissionObject from_server = 1;
}
message UpperCaseRequest {
    string original = 1;
}

message UpperCaseResponse {
    string upper_cased = 1;
}

service Transceiver {
    rpc Echo (EchoRequest) returns (EchoResponse);
    rpc UpperCase (UpperCaseRequest) returns (UpperCaseResponse);
}
```

Save the file to proto/transceiver.proto.

Note that all that was necessary was simply adding the new RPC declaration to the service, along with some explicit messages for the request and response.

Now let's add the implementation into the server. Open server/echo_server/echo_server.go.

Listing 8-9. Adding the implementation to the server

```go
import (
        "fmt"
        "log"
        "net"
        "strings"
        "transceiver"
        "transmission_object"

        "golang.org/x/net/context"
        "google.golang.org/grpc"
)
<omitted for brevity>
func (es *EchoServer) UpperCase(contest context.Context, request
*transceiver.UpperCaseRequest) (*transceiver.UpperCaseResponse, error) {
        log.Println("Original = " + (*request).GetOriginal())
        return &transceiver.UpperCaseResponse{
                UpperCased: strings.ToUpper((*request).GetOriginal()),
        }, nil
}

func main() {
        log.Println("Spinning up the Echo Server in Go...")
        listen, error := net.Listen("tcp", ":1234")
        if error != nil {
                log.Panicln("Unable to listen: " + error.Error())
        }
        defer listen.Close()
        defer log.Println("Connection now closed.")
```

```
grpc_server := grpc.NewServer()
transceiver.RegisterTransceiverServer(grpc_server, &EchoServer{})

error = grpc_server.Serve(listen)
if error != nil {
        log.Panicln("Unable to start serving! Error: " + error.Error())
}
}
```

Save the changes to server/echo_server/echo_server.go.

Once again, note that all that was necessary was adding in the new method to the struct.

Finally, let's make the modifications needed on the client side. Open client/echo_client/command_line/EchoClient.java.

Listing 8-10. Calling the new RPC from the client

```
import io.grpc.ManagedChannel;
import io.grpc.ManagedChannelBuilder;
import java.io.BufferedReader;
import java.io.InputStreamReader;

import transmission_object.TransmissionObjectOuterClass.TransmissionObject;
import transceiver.TransceiverOuterClass.EchoRequest;
import transceiver.TransceiverOuterClass.EchoResponse;
import transceiver.TransceiverOuterClass.UpperCaseRequest;
import transceiver.TransceiverOuterClass.UpperCaseResponse;
import transceiver.TransceiverGrpc;

public class EchoClient {
    public static void main(String args[]) {
        System.out.println("Spinning up the Echo Client in Java...");
        try {
```

<omitted for brevity>

```
                UpperCaseRequest upperCaseRequest =
                  UpperCaseRequest.newBuilder()
                    .setOriginal(inputFromUser)
                    .build();
                UpperCaseResponse upperCaseResponse =
                  stub.upperCase(upperCaseRequest);
                System.out.println("Received upper cased:");
                System.out.println(upperCaseResponse);

                channel.shutdownNow();
            }
        } catch (Exception e) {
            System.err.println("Error: " + e);
        }
    }
}
```

Save your changes to client/echo_client/command_line/EchoClient.java.

Once again, all that was needed was simple, to create the appropriate constructs and call the newly defined RPC. Let's run a test to verify that all is well.

Open a terminal and start the server:

```
chapter_08$ bazel run server/echo_server
INFO: Analysed target //server/echo_server:echo_server (1 packages loaded,
    594 targets configured).
INFO: Found 1 target...
Target //server/echo_server:echo_server up-to-date:
  bazel-bin/server/echo_server/darwin_amd64_stripped/echo_server
INFO: Elapsed time: 1.409s, Critical Path: 0.03s
INFO: 0 processes.
INFO: Build completed successfully, 1 total action
INFO: Build completed successfully, 1 total action
2019/07/23 05:40:16 Spinning up the Echo Server in Go...
```

Now open the client terminal, and let's run the client one more time:

```
chapter_08$ bazel run client/echo_client/command_line
INFO: Analysed target //client/echo_client/command_line:command_line
      (2 packages loaded, 432 targets configured).
INFO: Found 1 target...
Target //client/echo_client/command_line:command_line up-to-date:
  bazel-bin/client/echo_client/command_line/command_line.jar
  bazel-bin/client/echo_client/command_line/command_line
INFO: Elapsed time: 0.616s, Critical Path: 0.27s
INFO: 1 process: 1 worker.
INFO: Build completed successfully, 2 total actions
INFO: Build completed successfully, 2 total actions
Spinning up the Echo Client in Java...
Waiting on input from the user...
This is the magic.
Received Message from server:
from_server {
  value: 6.29
  message: "Received from client: This is the magic."
}

Received upper cased:
upper_cased: "THIS IS THE MAGIC."
```

Congratulations! You've just added a new RPC into your system. Notably, this required only a little bit more code in each location (definition, server, and client). Moving forward, you could easily define vastly more functionality in a very ordered and well-managed fashion.

Note   Within the body of this last section, we never made *any* modifications to our BUILD files, since no dependency changes were required. You were able to just operate on the code and execute, confident in the knowledge that Bazel would handle the necessary build steps.

Final Word

Over the course of the last chapter, the focus was less on an any structural knowledge on using Bazel than using it in a manner closer to actual development. You saw how Bazel's multi-language support worked hand in hand with gRPC to easily create new client–server functionality.

Up until this point in time in the book, the focus has been mainly on looking at functionality which effectively lives on a backend. That is, both the clients and servers created thus far could easily be proxies for backend services talking to one another.

Although much of the communication theme will continue moving forward, we will start to look at using Bazel to create purely client-side functionality in the form of mobile applications. Once again, we will lean heavily on Bazel's ability to work seamlessly across languages to create these applications.

CHAPTER 9

Bazel and Android

In the prior chapters, you used Bazel to develop functionality that would most likely be deployed to some backend server. However, Bazel can be (and is) used for more than just backend projects, able to handle mobile clients as well. In this chapter, we will explore using Bazel to build Android applications.

Setup

As previously, we will be building off of our prior chapters. Again, first verify that all of the Bazel-generated files are eliminated. Then, copy the work from the last chapter:

```
$ cd chapter_08
chapter_08$ bazel clean
chapter_08$ ls
WORKSPACE    client    proto    server

chapter_08$ cd ..
$ cp -rf chapter_08 chapter_09
$ cd chapter_09
chapter_09$
```

Workspace

As you might have already guessed, we need to augment our WORKSPACE file with an additional dependency. In this case, we are specifying the rules for building an Android project.

Open the WORKSPACE file and add the following.

© P.J. McNerney 2020
P.J. McNerney, *Beginning Bazel*, https://doi.org/10.1007/978-1-4842-5194-2_9

Listing 9-1. Modifying the WORKSPACE file for the Android rules

```
<existing content omitted for brevity>
http_archive(
    name = "rules_android",
    urls = ["https://github.com/bazelbuild/rules_android/archive/v0.1.1.zip"],
    strip_prefix = "rules_android-0.1.1",
)

android_sdk_repository(name = "androidsdk")
```

Note   In earlier chapters, we mentioned that there are certain rules that you get out of the box (e.g., java_library, cc_library, etc.). The rules for android_library and android_binary technically started as more *out-of-the-box* rules. However, as Bazel has matured, they have begun removing rules from this core set and creating explicit packages for these rules, for the sake of maintainability.

This should make sense from a development perspective; by making the rules more modular and less part of a monolithic package, they can be revised at their appropriate pace without requiring a rebuild of the entire Bazel system.

Within the *WORKSPACE* file, we are calling a rule android_sdk_repository. This is used to specify the path to the Android SDK with respect to this project. In this particular case, without any other additional specification within the rule itself, the rule defaults to using the *ANDROID_HOME* environment variable. We will set this shortly.

Note   The reliance on an environment variable in this case might set off some alarms, given Bazel's approach to maintaining control over its dependencies. In this particular case, the environment variable may be considered a convenience; however, it *is* possible to specify an explicit path to the Android SDKs, even relative to your current WORKSPACE file, within the android_sdk_repository rule.

This kind of specification is highly useful when you are checking Android SDK dependencies into source control. This once again returns Bazel to the type of hermetic build that it prefers.

Android Studio

In the course of this chapter, we are downloading Android Studio for the purpose of giving us an easy Android emulator on which to run our work as well as create a convenient location for the Android SDKs. Technically speaking, you *can* actually use the work you've done with Bazel to drive an Android Studio (and IntelliJ) project (akin to using something *gradle*). However, this integration is outside of the scope of this chapter of this book.

Note   To that end, you might either have a favorite Android emulator you prefer instead *or* want to just hook up your Android device to the computer to try this out. In these cases, you can largely skip using Android Studio (though please take particular care to make sure you have the Android SDKs you need as specified under the upcoming Environment section).

Go to `https://developer.android.com/studio` and follow the instructions for downloading and installing Android Studio on your particular platform.

The version of Android Studio used for the examples in this book is 3.4.2. Later versions may have visual changes, so the screenshots may not line up precisely.

Environment

As indicated previously, we need to set the `ANDROID_HOME` environment variable in order to ensure that Bazel knows where to find the Android SDKs. Make sure to set your `ANDROID_HOME` variable in your environment with the value pointing to the location of the Android SDK on your machine.

The default locations for the Android SDKs from Android Studio depends on the particular OS. Set the environment variables as appropriate to your system:

For Linux:

```
export ANDROID_HOME=$HOME/Android/Sdk/
```

For MacOS:

```
export ANDROID_HOME=$HOME/Library/Android/sdk
```

For Windows:

```
set ANDROID_HOME=%LOCALAPPDATA%\Android\Sdk
```

One thing to note is that the preceding commands will only set the environment variable for the lifetime of your particular console session. You may want to consider making these a part of the default profile for your particular console and OS.

Additionally, the preceding values are only the *default* locations for the SDK; it is possible that during the course of installation of Android Studio, you may have installed into a different location. In order to find that location, open the SDK Manager in Android Studio.

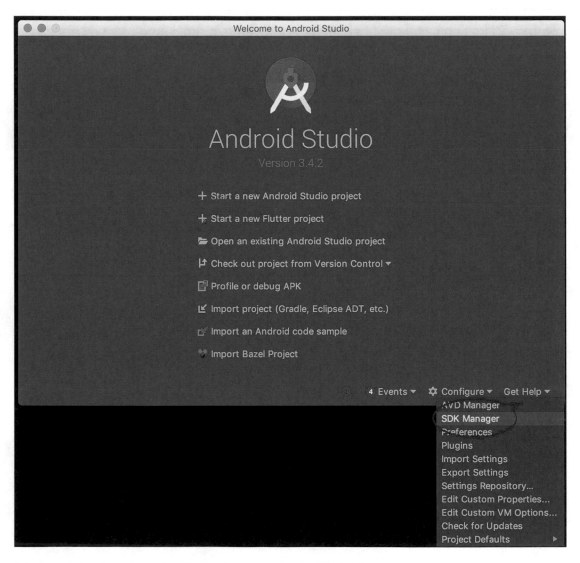

Figure 9-1. *Starting the SDK Manager in Android Studio*

Within the SDK Manager, you will be able to find the location of the Android SDK. Use that value to set the value of the ANDROID_HOME environment variable.

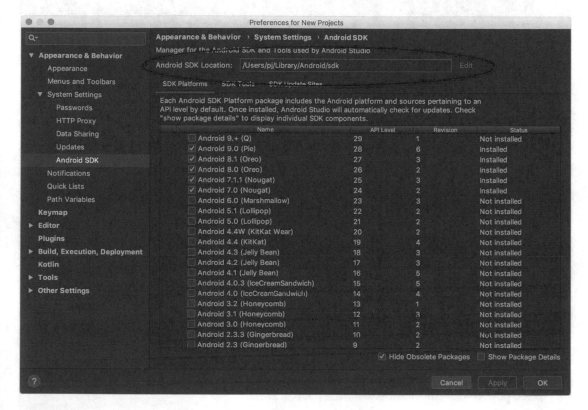

Figure 9-2. *Verifying the location of the Android SDK*

Downloading SDKs

While we have the SDK Manager up and running, we should also ensure that we have at least one Android SDK to begin development. Select at least *Android 8.1 (Oreo)* (i.e., API Level 27) and then click *OK* to begin downloading the SDKs (if you have selected more than one).

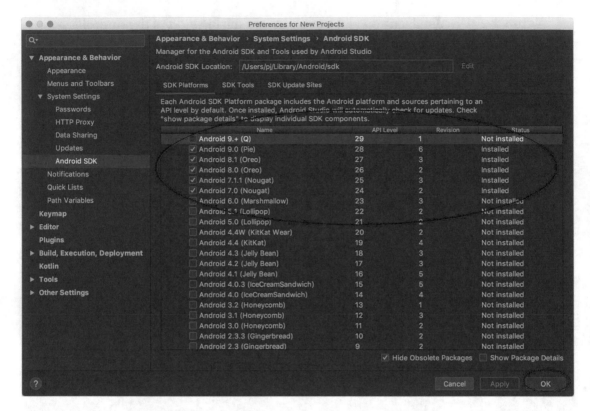

Figure 9-3. *Selecting versions of the Android SDK to download*

Once you've downloaded the SDK(s), click *Finish*.

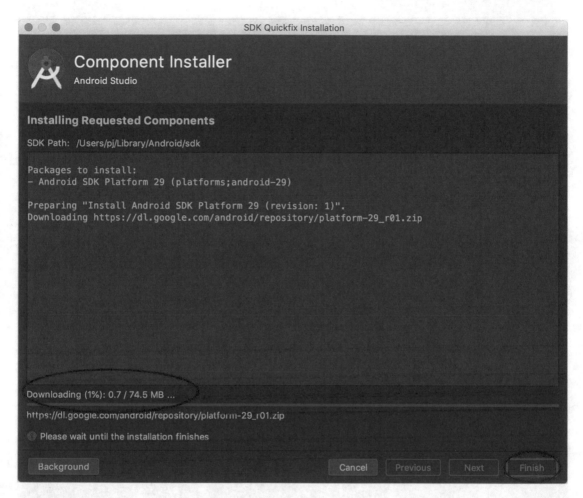

Figure 9-4. Downloading the Android SDKs

Creating the Emulator

Finally, let's create an instance of the Android Emulator. From the main screen, open the *AVD Manager*.

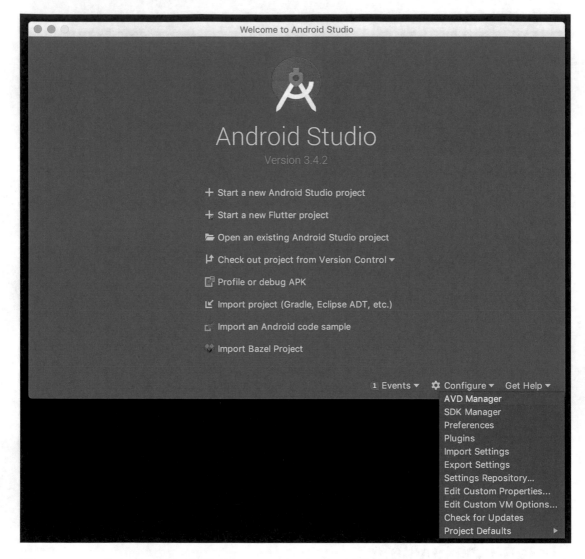

Figure 9-5. *Starting the AVD Manager in Android Studio*

At this point, we don't have any emulator profiles, so let's create one by clicking *Create Virtual Device.*

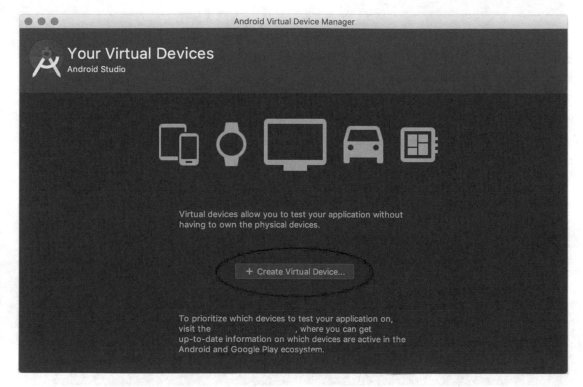

Figure 9-6. *Creating a virtual device*

From the *Select Hardware* screen, select a device (e.g., Pixel 2) from the Phone category and then click *Next*.

Figure 9-7. *Selecting a particular device*

From the *System Image* screen, select the particular version (e.g., Oreo) of the Android SDK that you want to use and then click *Next*.

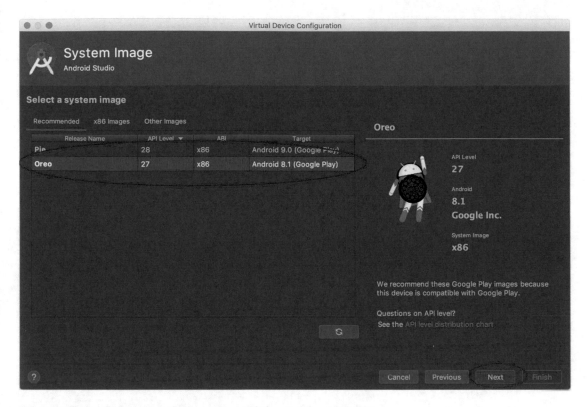

Figure 9-8. *Selecting the version of the Android SDK*

Finally, you can give your particular emulation profile a name (if you would like). Click *Finish* to complete the creation of your virtual device.

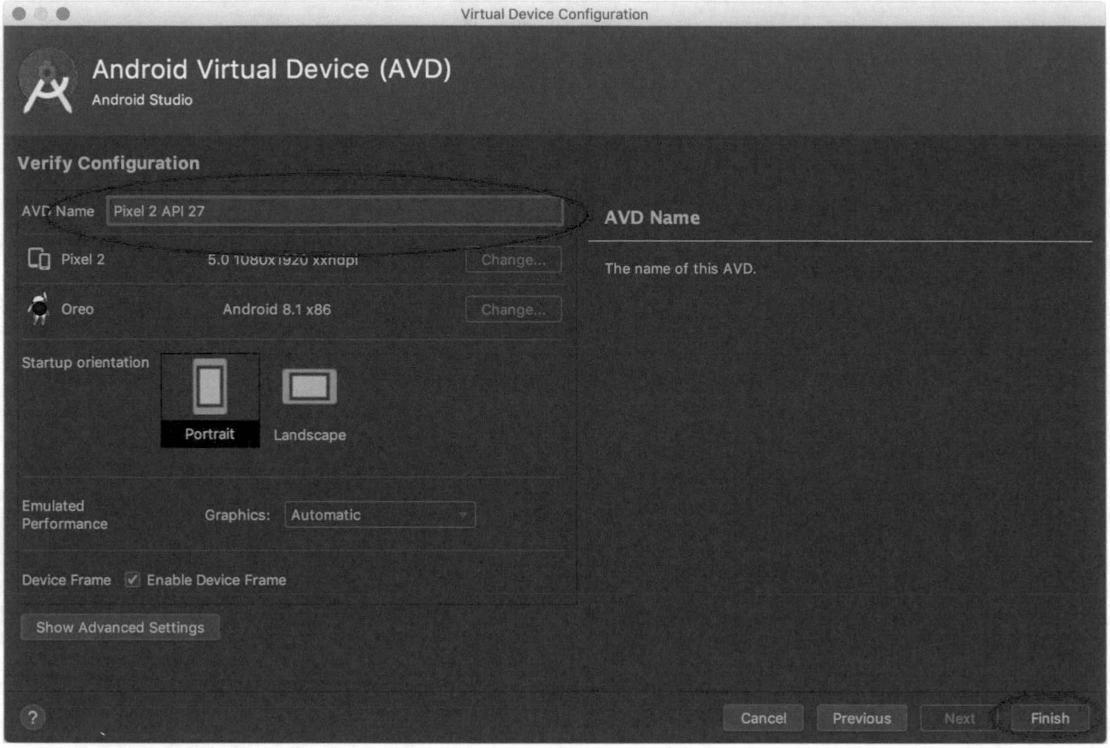

Figure 9-9. *Naming and completing the virtual device*

Creating the Android Echo Client in Bazel

Having done all the preparation, we are now ready to start actually creating our Android application. In this case, we are going to create a mobile version of our echo client.

However, before we get to the actual gRPC code, we'll start with a simple shell version that just echoes locally (i.e., input text returns immediately). This is simply to get used to the basics of developing an Android application in Bazel.

Let's create a new directory for our Android work:

```
chapter_09$ cd client/echo_client/
chapter_09/client/echo_client$ mkdir android
chapter_09/client/echo_client$ cd android
chapter_09/client/echo_client/android$
```

Within the client/echo_client/android directory, create the EchoClientMainActivity.java file and add the following.

Listing 9-2. Creating a basic Android echo client

```
package client.echo_client.android;

import android.app.Activity;
import android.os.Bundle;
import android.view.View;
import android.widget.Button;
import android.widget.EditText;
import android.widget.TextView;

public class EchoClientMainActivity extends Activity {
    @Override
    public void onCreate(Bundle savedInstanceState) {
        super.onCreate(savedInstanceState);

        setContentView(R.layout.echo_client_main_activity);

        Button textSenderButton = findViewById(R.id.text_sender);
        EditText clientTextEditor = findViewById(R.id.text_input);
        TextView serverResultsText = findViewById(R.id.server_result_text);

        textSenderButton.setOnClickListener(new View.OnClickListener() {
            public void onClick(View v) {
                serverResultsText.setText(clientTextEditor.getText().
                toString());
            }});
    }
}
```

Save the file to EchoClientMainActivity.java. As evidenced in the preceding code, we are creating a simple text editor to input text; upon the push of the button, the text is then reflected in a text view.

Now let's create the layout file that actually creates the UI:

```
chapter_09/client/echo_client/android$ mkdir -p res/layout
```

Create the following file under client/echo_client/android/res/layout.

Listing 9-3. Creating the layout file

```xml
<?xml version="1.0" encoding="utf-8"?>
<LinearLayout xmlns:android="http://schemas.android.com/apk/res/android"
    android:orientation="vertical"
    android:gravity="top"
    android:layout_width="match_parent"
    android:layout_height="match_parent">

  <EditText
    android:id="@+id/text_input"
    android:layout_height="wrap_content"
    android:layout_width="match_parent"
    android:inputType="text"/>

  <Button
      android:id="@+id/text_sender"
      android:layout_width="wrap_content"
      android:layout_height="wrap_content"
      android:layout_gravity="center_horizontal"
      android:text="Send to Server"/>

  <TextView
      android:id="@+id/server_result_text"
      android:layout_width="wrap_content"
      android:layout_height="wrap_content"
      android:layout_gravity="center_horizontal"
      android:inputType="textMultiLine"
      android:text="Result text here"/>
</LinearLayout>
```

Save the file to echo_client_main_activity.xml under client/echo_client/
android/res/layout.

For our Android app, we also need an AndroidManifest.xml file.

Listing 9-4. AndroidManifest.xml

```
<manifest xmlns:android="http://schemas.android.com/apk/res/android"
    package="client.echo_client.android"
    android:versionCode="1"
    android:versionName="1.0" >

  <uses-sdk
      android:minSdkVersion="19"
      android:targetSdkVersion="27" />

  <application
    android:label="Beginning Bazel Android Echo Client">
    <activity
        android:name=".EchoClientMainActivity"
        android:label="Beginning Bazel Android Echo Client" >
        <intent-filter>
            <action android:name="android.intent.action.MAIN" />
            <category android:name="android.intent.category.LAUNCHER" />
        </intent-filter>
    </activity>
  </application>
</manifest>
```

Save this to client/echo_client/android/AndroidManifest.xml.

Finally, let's create our BUILD file and define our targets.

Listing 9-5. Creating the BUILD file for the Android client

```
load("@rules_android//android:rules.bzl", "android_library", "android_binary")
android_library(
    name = "echo_client_android_activity",
    srcs = ["EchoClientMainActivity.java"],
    manifest = "AndroidManifest.xml",
    custom_package = "client.echo_client.android",
    resource_files = [
        "res/layout/echo_client_main_activity.xml"
    ],
```

```
)
android_binary(
    name = "echo_client_android_app",
    manifest = "AndroidManifest.xml",
    custom_package = "client.echo_client.android",
    deps = [ ":echo_client_android_activity",],

)
```

Save this to `client/echo_client/android/BUILD`.

Although the Android build rules are new, you have seen this pattern several times throughout this book. As expected, we needed to explicitly load the `android_library` and `android_binary` rules from the `rules_android` package.

For the each of the rules, there are a number of attributes that are familiar (i.e., name, srcs, dep). There are a few attributes worth highlighting:

- manifest

  - Points at the `AndroidManifest.xml` file.

  - Required for both `android_library` and `android_binary`.

- resource_files

  - Contains the set of Android resource files (e.g., layout.xml, strings.xml, etc.).

  - Strictly speaking, this is *optional*; however, in this particular example, removing this attribute here will cause the build to fail (since it no longer depends upon the files required for the generated classes).

- custom_package

  - This explicitly specifies the package used by the app.

  - Both `android_library` and `android_binary` have an expectation about the directory structure.

- Specifically, they expect that the directory starts with either java or javatests as a way of inferring the Java package.

- If the directory does *not* start with java, then it is necessary to explicitly set the custom_package attribute.

Now, technically speaking, we did not strictly need to have both an android_library instance and an android_binary instance. The android_binary rule actually has a sufficient set of options that we *could* have put everything (i.e., Java sources and resource files) we needed there. However, the separation here is intended to illustrate both rules.

Let's run a test build to make sure that everything is working as intended. For the sake of simplicity, we will just build the final binary:

```
chapter_09/client/echo_client/android$ bazel build :echo_client_android_app
INFO: Analyzed target //client/echo_client/android:echo_client_android_app
      (1 packages loaded, 5 targets configured).
INFO: Found 1 target...
Target //client/echo_client/android:echo_client_android_app up-to-date:
  bazel-bin/client/echo_client/android/echo_client_android_app_deploy.jar
  bazel-bin/client/echo_client/android/echo_client_android_app_unsigned.apk
  bazel-bin/client/echo_client/android/echo_client_android_app.apk
INFO: Elapsed time: 0.935s, Critical Path: 0.70s
INFO: 3 processes: 3 darwin-sandbox.
INFO: Build completed successfully, 4 total actions
```

Congratulations! You have built your first Android application using Bazel. We are now ready to test it out on the emulator.

Starting Up the Android Emulator Instance

Having previously created your virtual device, you can now start it up. Open the *AVD Manager*, which will now have a listing of all your virtual devices (in this example, there is only one). Click the "play" button to start up an instance of your virtual device.

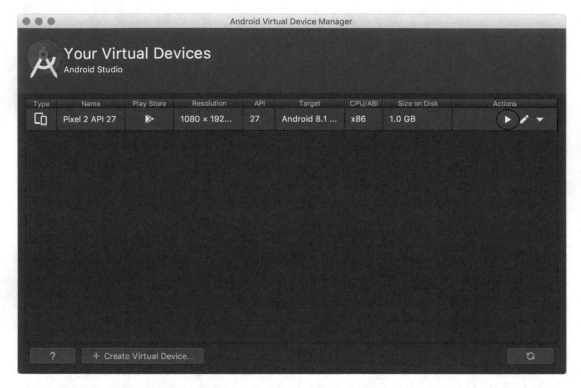

Figure 9-10. *Starting the virtual device*

You should see a blank screen as follows.

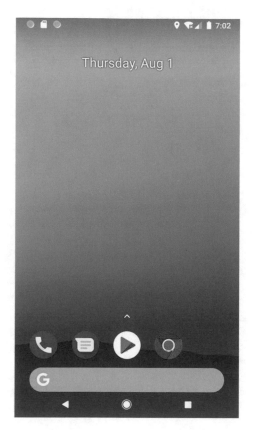

Figure 9-11. *Emulator after start-up*

Bazel Mobile Install

Having built and set up our emulator, we are now ready to deploy our application. On first blush, we could make use of the Android Debug Bridge (ADB) commands to get our application onto the emulator. However, Bazel provides a very useful command `mobile-install`. In a similar fashion to `run`, `mobile-install` builds the target application and then installs onto the connected device (in this case, the emulator).

As an added bonus, we can also add the option `start_app` in order to immediately start the app as soon as it is installed. Using this option makes `mobile-install` a functional mobile equivalent to `run` used in prior chapters.

Run the following command to build, deploy, and start the application:

```
chapter_09/client/echo_client/android$ bazel mobile-install --start_app
:echo_client_android_app
```

Figure 9-12. *Initial screen of the app*

Congratulations! Your application is alive and will locally echo whatever you write into the text editor.

Note   The *mobile-install* command is not just a convenient proxy for the ADB functionality. Since it is tied into the Bazel build system, it can also be used for deploying incremental changes to your mobile applications. This can greatly improve your development times, allowing you to take a more iterative approach to working on various aspects of the mobile application (e.g., the UI). However, the particulars around using this incremental deployment are outside of the scope of this book.

Adding gRPC Support

While the prior example was useful for creating a basic Android application, it is not a very functional app. Carrying over our theme from prior chapters, let's now add the real echo client functionality to this application. Fortunately, you have already done the heavy lifting in prior chapters; we get to reuse that here.

Before we jump into the Android code itself, we have to first make sure we add the appropriate permission; otherwise, we will get errors when we attempt to perform interprocess communication.

Open the `AndroidManifest.xml` file and add the following permission.

Listing 9-6. Adding permission to access networking to the Android app

```xml
<manifest xmlns:android="http://schemas.android.com/apk/res/android"
    package="client.echo_client.android"
    android:versionCode="1"
    android:versionName="1.0" >

  <uses-sdk
      android:minSdkVersion="19"
      android:targetSdkVersion="27" />

  <uses-permission android:name="android.permission.INTERNET"/>

  <application
    android:label="Beginning Bazel Android Echo Client">
    <activity
        android:name=".EchoClientMainActivity"
        android:label="Beginning Bazel Android Echo Client" >
        <intent-filter>
            <action android:name="android.intent.action.MAIN" />
            <category android:name="android.intent.category.LAUNCHER" />
        </intent-filter>
    </activity>
  </application>
</manifest>
```

Save the changes to `AndroidManifest.xml`.

Now let's make the necessary changes to the Android code itself. Open the `EchoClientMainActivity.java` file and add the following changes in bold.

Listing 9-7. Modifying the Android client to support gRPC

```java
package java.com.beginning_bazel.client.echo_client;

import android.app.Activity;
import android.os.Bundle;
import android.util.Log;
import android.view.View;
import android.widget.Button;
import android.widget.EditText;
import android.widget.TextView;

import io.grpc.ManagedChannel;
import io.grpc.ManagedChannelBuilder;

import transmission_object.TransmissionObjectOuterClass.TransmissionObject;
import transceiver.TransceiverOuterClass.EchoRequest;
import transceiver.TransceiverOuterClass.EchoResponse;
import transceiver.TransceiverGrpc;

public class EchoClientMainActivity extends Activity {
    @Override
    public void onCreate(Bundle savedInstanceState) {
        super.onCreate(savedInstanceState);

        setContentView(R.layout.echo_client_main_activity);

        Button textSenderButton = findViewById(R.id.text_sender);
        EditText clientTextEditor = findViewById(R.id.text_input);
        TextView serverResultsText = findViewById(R.id.server_result_text);

        textSenderButton.setOnClickListener(new View.OnClickListener() {
            public void onClick(View v) {
                final String clientText =
                    clientTextEditor.getText().toString();
                if (!clientText.isEmpty()) {
                    ManagedChannel channel =
                        ManagedChannelBuilder
```

```
                .forAddress("10.0.2.2", 1234)
                .usePlaintext()
                .build();
        TransceiverGrpc.TransceiverBlockingStub stub =
            TransceiverGrpc.newBlockingStub(channel);
        EchoRequest request = EchoRequest.newBuilder()
          .setFromClient(
              TransmissionObject.newBuilder()
                .setMessage(clientText)
                .setValue(3.145f)
                .build();
          .build();
        try {
            EchoResponse response = stub.echo(request);
            serverResultsText.setText(response.toString());
        } catch (Throwable t) {
            Log.d("EchoClientMainActivity", "error:", t);
        } finally {
            channel.shutdown();
        }
      }
    }});
  }
}
```

Save the changes to EchoClientMainActivity.java.

Note   A careful reader will note that we have changed the address from *localhost* to *10.0.2.2*. Within the emulator *localhost* refers to the emulated device, rather than the machine the emulator is running on. Android Studio designates a special IP address (i.e., *10.0.2.2*) in order to connect to processes running on your development machine. You don't need to change anything on the server side.

Should one decide to use a *different* emulation platform, please consult with that platform's documentation to see if it designates a different address (or uses a different strategy) in order to connect to processes running on your development machine.

All of the added code should look familiar to you; with only a couple of changes, it is identical to the code on the command line Java client from the previous chapter.

Note   In both the last chapter and this one, we are making use of the *blocking stub* version for calling into the backend. Although convenient for us here, in general, you would not want to make such an I/O call on a UI thread, since such a call could make the UI unresponsive. Instead, you likely would want to investigate some of the other generated versions (e.g., using a Future) of this call as a best fit for your application.

Finally, let's add the necessary dependencies to the BUILD file. Once again, this should look very familiar to you, with few changes from the prior chapter.

Listing 9-8. Adding dependencies into the Android BUILD file

```
load("@rules_android//android:rules.bzl", "android_library", "android_binary")
android_library(
    name = "echo_client_android_activity",
    srcs = ["EchoClientMainActivity.java"],
    manifest = "AndroidManifest.xml",
    custom_package = "client.echo_client.android",
    resource_files = [
        "res/layout/echo_client_main_activity.xml"
    ],
    deps = [
        "//proto:transceiver_java_proto",
        "//proto:transceiver_java_proto_grpc",
        "//proto:transmission_object_java_proto",
        "@io_grpc_grpc_java//api",
        "@io_grpc_grpc_java//okhttp",
        "@io_grpc_grpc_java//stub",
    ],
)

android_binary(
    name = "echo_client_android_app",
```

```
    manifest = "AndroidManifest.xml",
    deps = [ ":echo_client_android_activity",],
)
```

Note   Once again, an astute reader will see that we have replaced our former
@io_grpc_grpc_java//netty runtime dependency with the @io_grpc_
grpc_java/okhttp static dependency. To be sure, netty is most appropriate
for supporting both client *and* server functionality. OkHttp is designed to be
lightweight for client-only, hence its inclusion into Android here.

Save the changes to the BUILD file.

For sanity's sake, let's build the app once more. However, you might get a surprising
error message this time.

```
chapter_09/client/echo_client/android$ bazel build :echo_client_android_app
ERROR: <stack trace>
'single_file' is no longer supported. use allow_single_file instead. You
can use --incompatible_disable_deprecated_attr_params=false to temporarily
disable this check.
ERROR: <file_path>/external/io_grpc_grpc_java/protobuf-lite/BUILD.
bazel:1:1: error loading package '@com_google_protobuf_javalite//':
Extension file 'protobuf.bzl' has errors and referenced by '@io_grpc_grpc_
java//protobuf-lite:protobuf-lite'
ERROR: Analysis of target '//client/echo_client/android:echo_client_
android_app' failed; build aborted: error loading package '@com_google_
protobuf_javalite//': Extension file 'protobuf.bzl' has errors
```

In this particular case, you haven't done anything wrong; you might have run into
this error due to the evolving nature of Bazel. In this case, one of your dependencies has
an error due to a deprecated attribute. All is not lost, however, and the highlighted line
above gives us an answer as to how to proceed.

If we add in the flag --incompatible_disable_deprecated_attr_params=false to
the build (and mobile-install) command, you can see the issue correct itself.

```
chapter_09/client/echo_client/android$ bazel build --incompatible_disable_
deprecated_attr_params=false :echo_client_android_app
INFO: Writing tracer profile to '/private/var/tmp/_bazel_pj/72676801ec24996
691dac393febb05db/command.profile.gz'
INFO: Analyzed target //client/echo_client/android:echo_client_android_app
(80 packages loaded, 2140 targets configured).
INFO: Found 1 target...
Target //client/echo_client/android:echo_client_android_app up-to-date:
  bazel-bin/client/echo_client/android/echo_client_android_app_deploy.jar
  bazel-bin/client/echo_client/android/echo_client_android_app_unsigned.apk
  bazel-bin/client/echo_client/android/echo_client_android_app.apk
INFO: Elapsed time: 11.048s, Critical Path: 6.06s
INFO: 13 processes: 9 darwin-sandbox, 4 worker.
INFO: Build completed successfully, 14 total actions
```

Strictly speaking, although this works, this should not be considered a permanent solution. When you actually encounter something like this, the correct solution will be to fix the problem in the dependency (possibly submitting a change for it). This also illustrates the advantage of keeping your advantages as local as possible, to make it easier to control your own destiny.

One thing this does illustrate, however, is that Bazel, even in its own rapid evolution, seeks to provide you with "escape valves" to keep development moving forward. While not permanent solutions, these do enable you to more easily transition between versions of the software.

Running the Android Client Against the Backend

Having augmented our Android client to make RPCs against a local server, let's now start both the server and the client up.

Previously, you needed two console instances, since your client and server were both command line tools. Here, you will be able to use just one.

First, let's build, deploy, and start our updated Android app. Run the following command:

```
bazel mobile-install --incompatible_disable_deprecated_attr_params=false
--start_app :echo_client_android_app
```

After confirming that the application is up and running, run the following command to start the server:

```
chapter_09$ bazel run server/echo_server
INFO: Deleting stale sandbox base /private/var/tmp/_bazel_pj/72676801ec2499
    6691dac393febb05db/sandbox
Target //server/echo_server:echo_server up-to-date:
  bazel-bin/server/echo_server/darwin_amd64_stripped/echo_server
INFO: Elapsed time: 16.670s, Critical Path: 0.30s
INFO: 0 processes.
INFO: Build completed successfully, 1 total action
INFO: Build completed successfully, 1 total action
2019/08/01 16:39:03 Spinning up the Echo Server in Go
```

Now, write up some text and click "Send to Server." You should get a response in your Android client, as follows.

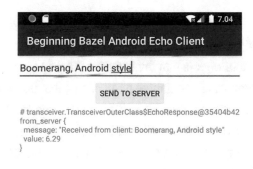

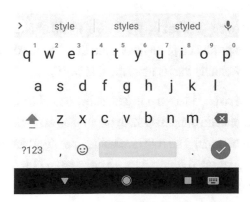

Figure 9-13. *Screen showcasing the app with displayed response from the backend*

161

Congratulations! You have created your Android echo client, communicating with the local echo server.

Final Word

Over the course of the latest chapter, you augmented your knowledge by learning how to build Android applications using Bazel. Furthermore, you were able to take what you have learned in earlier chapters to create an application that communicated with the work you've done previously. Although this is clearly a toy example of remote communication, it serves as a seed for larger projects.

Having demonstrated Bazel's ability to work with building Android project, we will expand in the next chapter to also work on iOS applications.

EXERCISE – USING JAVA LITE PROTOS ON ANDROID

Over the course of the last chapter, you were able to make use of your work from earlier chapters to easily add gRPC support to your Android application. One note that was glossed over during the course of this work is that the output of the `java_proto_library` tends to be rather verbose in terms of sheer number of functions; that is, the number of generated classes, inner classes, static classes, and so on tends to be large. While this is less of an issue for programs that run on servers, this actually starts to become an issue at scale for Android programs. Veterans of writing Android programs are familiar with the dreaded function count within a single DEX file (i.e., 64K functions).

Although you can adopt a multidex strategy to handle this increased number of functions, this can become complicated depending on the version of the Android SDK. Fortunately, at least in the case of the `java_proto_library`, we have a viable alternative in the `java_lite_proto_library`. This rule produces proto Java code that has fewer overall features, while still retaining the core functionality that is used most of the time.

Notably, the `java_lite_proto_library` is (currently) one of those out-of-the-box rules which also requires some outside support (which might give an indication about the migration path for this particular set of rules). The rule is specified nearly *identically* to the `java_proto_library`. Protos generated from `java_lite_proto_library` do not implement *all* of the functionality of the original version but can be often used as drop-in replacements for the most common use cases (as is the case here).

Fortunately, you can easily get the support you need by adding the following lines to your WORKSPACE file:

```
http_archive(
    name = "com_google_protobuf_javalite",
    strip_prefix = "protobuf-javalite",
    urls = ["https://github.com/google/protobuf/archive/javalite.zip"],
)
```

To that end, you will also need to ensure that the grpc library that you are using *also* produces code that is compatible with the output of the java_lite_proto_library. Fortunately, our existing rule of java_grpc_library already handles this for us; all you need to do is to add the option flavor = "lite" to the application.

For example:

```
java_grpc_library(
    name = "transceiver_java_lite_proto_grpc",
    srcs = [":transceiver_proto"],
    deps = [":transceiver_java_lite_proto"],
    flavor = "lite",
    visibility = ["//client/echo_client:__subpackages__"],
)
```

Once you've created your java_lite_proto_library and java_grpc_library (with "lite" proto support) instances, redirect your app's android_library to point at these newly created rules. The way we are using protobufs in this instance means you don't have to change any of your Android code. You should be able to build and run the code, with no functional change.

However, you should look at the size of your app before/after this change. You should see a significant reduction in size (and if you really want to know the difference, use Android Studio's profiling tool to see the difference in the number of functions).

For toy projects, this difference will not amount to much; however, as you grow your Android apps to significant sizes using protobufs, you will want to make use of the "lite" versions to help keep your application sizes small and avoid the use of multidex.

CHAPTER 10

Bazel and iOS

In the previous chapter, you made use of Bazel to expand from command line programs, suitable for servers, and leaped into the mobile world through Android. To complete the work, we will create an equivalent client for iOS.

Note   In this chapter, we are going to be creating an iOS project using the native tools. However, since Xcode is only available on MacOS, you will only be able to build this chapter's project on an MacOS machine.

Setup

Once again, we will be building off of our prior chapters. Verify that the prior chapter's Bazel-generated files are eliminated; then copy the prior work:

```
$ cd chapter_09
chapter_09$ bazel clean
chapter_09$ ls
WORKSPACE    client    proto    server

chapter_09$ cd ..
$ cp -rf chapter_09 chapter_10
$ cd chapter_10
chapter_10$
```

Since you have already set up Xcode on your machine to build the examples in the prior chapters, you should have everything that you need for developing your iOS application.

© P.J. McNerney 2020
P.J. McNerney, *Beginning Bazel*, https://doi.org/10.1007/978-1-4842-5194-2_10

Workspace

Once again, we will add in dependencies to our WORKSPACE file to retrieve the rules required for building an iOS project.

Open the WORKSPACE file and add the following.

Listing 10-1. Modifying the WORKSPACE for the iOS rules

```
load("@bazel_tools//tools/build_defs/repo:http.bzl", "http_archive")
load("@bazel_tools//tools/build_defs/repo:git.bzl", "git_repository")

skylib_version = "0.8.0"

http_archive(
    name = "bazel_skylib",
    url = "https://github.com/bazelbuild/bazel-skylib/releases/download/{}/
    bazel-skylib.{}.tar.gz".format(skylib_version, skylib_version),
)

git_repository(
    name ="build_bazel_rules_apple",
    commit="1445924a158a89ad634f562c84a600a3435ef8c2",
    remote="https://github.com/bazelbuild/rules_apple.git",
)

load(
    "@build_bazel_rules_apple//apple:repositories.bzl",
    "apple_rules_dependencies",
)

apple_rules_dependencies()

load(
    "@build_bazel_rules_swift//swift:repositories.bzl",
    "swift_rules_dependencies",
)
```

```
swift_rules_dependencies()

load(
    "@build_bazel_apple_support//lib:repositories.bzl",
    "apple_support_dependencies",
)

apple_support_dependencies()
<existing content omitted for brevity>
```

Save your changes to the *WORKSPACE* file.

Note   In these particular changes, we are only explicitly calling into `http_`
`archive` for the `build_bazel_rules_apple`; however, we are clearly getting
multiple additional dependencies through the `*_dependencies()` functions. You
have seen this in earlier chapters, but it is worth calling out since we will explicitly
use rules from one of these additional packages (i.e., the `build_bazel_rules_`
`swift` package).

Creating the iOS Client in Bazel

Similar to what you wrote under the Android example, we will start by creating a basic
iOS application, ahead of actually employing any gRPC code. Along the way, we will
explore a few of the fine points for building iOS applications under Bazel.

Let's create a new directory for our iOS work. As expected, it will live within the client
directory, adjacent to the Android and command line clients:

```
chapter_10$ cd client/echo_client/
chapter_10/client/echo_client$ mkdir ios
chapter_10/client/echo_client$ cd ios
chapter_10/client/echo_client/ios$
```

Within the `client/echo_client/ios` directory, create the `MainViewController.`
`swift` file and add the following.

Listing 10-2. Creating the MainViewController

```swift
import UIKit

public class MainViewController : UIViewController {

    private let textInput = UITextField()
    private let sendButton =  UIButton(type: UIButton.ButtonType.system)
    private let receivedText = UILabel()

    override public func viewDidLoad() {
        super.viewDidLoad()

        self.view.backgroundColor = .white

        textInput.placeholder = "Input text here"
        textInput.textColor = .black
        textInput.backgroundColor =.white
        textInput.isEnabled = true

        sendButton.setTitle("Send", for: UIControl.State.normal)
        sendButton.addTarget(self, action: #selector(send), for:
        .touchUpInside)
        sendButton.isEnabled = true

        receivedText.numberOfLines = 0
        receivedText.text = "Received text will show up here."
        receivedText.backgroundColor = .gray
        receivedText.textColor = .black

        let stackView = UIStackView(arrangedSubviews: [self.textInput,
        self.sendButton, self.receivedText])
        stackView.alignment = .fill
        stackView.axis = .vertical
        stackView.distribution = .fillEqually
        stackView.spacing = 10.0
        stackView.translatesAutoresizingMaskIntoConstraints = false

        self.view.addSubview(stackView)
    }
```

```
override public func viewDidAppear(_ animated: Bool) {
    super.viewDidAppear(animated)
    textInput.text = ""
    receivedText.text = ""
}

@objc func send(sender: UIButton!) {
    receivedText.text = textInput.text
}
}
```

Save the file to `MainViewController.swift`. As we did with the Android version of the client, we are creating a very simple local echo client, which just reflects the input text to an output upon clicking *Send*.

Note   Unlike the Android client, we are programmatically generating the UI through code, rather than creating an equivalent `.storyboard` file. Although the Bazel rules for iOS do support using `.storyboard` files, the standard tool for generating these files is Xcode itself (i.e., through the creation of a new project). For the sake of simplicity, we choose to forego using a `.storyboard` file, since the code for generating the UI is very straightforward.

In the Android example, we defined all of our application within a single file; here, we will create one more (i.e., the AppDelegate file) in order to follow iOS convention.

Within the `client/echo_client/ios` directory, create the `AppDelegate.swift` file and add the following.

Listing 10-3. Creating the basic AppDelegate

```
import UIKit

@UIApplicationMain
class AppDelegate: NSObject, UIApplicationDelegate {
    var window: UIWindow?

    func application(
        _ application: UIApplication, didFinishLaunchingWithOptions
        launchOptions: [UIApplication.LaunchOptionsKey : Any]?) -> Bool {
```

169

```
        window = UIWindow(frame: UIScreen.main.bounds)
        window?.makeKeyAndVisible()
        window?.rootViewController = MainViewController()
        return true
    }
}
```

Save the file to `AppDelegate.swift`.

Finally, we will need to create an `Info.plist` file to define some of the basic attributes for our iOS application.

Within the `client/echo_client/ios` directory, create the `Info.plist` file and add the following.

Listing 10-4. Creating the Info.plist file

```
<?xml version="1.0" encoding="UTF-8"?>
<!DOCTYPE plist PUBLIC "-//Apple//DTD PLIST 1.0//EN" "http://www.apple.com/
DTDs/PropertyList-1.0.dtd">
<plist version="1.0">
<dict>
    <key>CFBundleDevelopmentRegion</key>
    <string>en</string>
    <key>CFBundleExecutable</key>
    <string>$(EXECUTABLE_NAME)</string>
    <key>CFBundleIdentifier</key>
    <string>$(PRODUCT_BUNDLE_IDENTIFIER)</string>
    <key>CFBundleInfoDictionaryVersion</key>
    <string>6.0</string>
    <key>CFBundleName</key>
    <string>$(PRODUCT_NAME)</string>
    <key>CFBundlePackageType</key>
    <string>APPL</string>
    <key>CFBundleShortVersionString</key>
    <string>1.0</string>
    <key>CFBundleVersion</key>
    <string>1</string>
    <key>LSRequiresIPhoneOS</key>
```

```
    <true/>
    <key>UIRequiredDeviceCapabilities</key>
    <array>
        <string>arm64</string>
    </array>
    <key>UISupportedInterfaceOrientations</key>
    <array>
        <string>UIInterfaceOrientationPortrait</string>
    </array>
</dict>
</plist>
```

Save the file to Info.plist.

Within client/echo_client/ios directory, create a BUILD file and add the following to it.

Listing 10-5. Creating the BUILD file for the iOS project

```
load("@build_bazel_rules_apple//apple:ios.bzl", "ios_application")
load("@build_bazel_rules_swift//swift:swift.bzl", "swift_library")

swift_library(
    name = "Lib",
    srcs = [
        "AppDelegate.swift",
        "MainViewController.swift",
    ],
)

ios_application(
    name = "EchoClient",
    bundle_id = "com.beginning-bazel.echo-client",
    families = ["iphone"],
    infoplists = [":Info.plist"],
    minimum_os_version = "11.0",
    deps = [":Lib"],
)
```

Save the BUILD file.

Given the work from prior chapters, nothing in the BUILD file should feel very foreign; you've simply loaded up a new set of rules and used them to create some build targets. In particular, swift_library should seem very familiar to similar instances in other languages. For the ios_application, many of the attributes are new, but also should make sense.

Building for iOS

Having set up our code and BUILD rules, let's now execute a build. Let's start with the EchoClient target:

```
chapter_10/client/echo_client/ios$ bazel build :EchoClient
INFO: Analyzed target //client/echo_client/ios:EchoClient (19 packages
      loaded, 405 targets configured).
INFO: Found 1 target...
Target //client/echo_client/ios:EchoClient up-to-date:
  bazel-bin/client/echo_client/ios/EchoClient.ipa
INFO: Elapsed time: 9.965s, Critical Path: 9.48s
INFO: 10 processes: 7 darwin-sandbox, 2 local, 1 worker.
INFO: Build completed successfully, 36 total actions
```

Once again, this should look very familiar from prior chapters.

However, let's also perform a build on the Lib target. Although we have effectively successfully built this target as a dependency of EchoClient, it is worthwhile to have a discussion around having sufficient context to build a target.

```
chapter_10/client/echo_client/ios$ bazel build :Lib
INFO: Analyzed target //client/echo_client/ios:Lib (25 packages loaded, 854
      targets configured).
INFO: Found 1 target...
ERROR: chapter_10/client/echo_client/ios/BUILD:4:1: Compiling Swift module
      client_echo_client_ios_Lib failed (Exit 1)
client/echo_client/ios/AppDelegate.swift:1:8: error: no such module 'UIKit'
import UIKit
       ^
Target //client/echo_client/ios:Lib failed to build
```

```
Use --verbose_failures to see the command lines of failed build steps.
INFO: Elapsed time: 4.094s, Critical Path: 0.15s
INFO: 0 processes.
FAILED: Build did NOT complete successfully
```

Although we have correctly set up the build targets, the build *fails*, with an error that should seem strange. After all, UIKit is a core library for iOS applications; it is always available when building an iOS application.

To understand what is going on, let us recall that Swift, as a language, is not bound to only building for iOS; you can create a native application via Swift for many platforms. Our initial specification within the BUILD file simply used swift_library; this alone gives no information as to what platform the Swift library should be built. Indeed, by default, it would be built for the MacOS platform (i.e., the system default).

In the case of ios_application, we are explicitly stating that this target should be *cross-compiled* for the iOS platform, pulling in the appropriate SDKs required to properly compile. Bazel has a property called *configuration* which encapsulates the environment's information when performing a build. By default, the configuration from a build target will be applied to the dependencies. This is why you were able to successfully build all of EchoClient earlier, since the ios_application had the proper configuration and this applied to the dependencies.

To enable this for the *swift_library* alone, we can add some specification to the *build* command in order to properly execute.

Execute the following, which adds the directive --apple_platform_type=ios to the command line:

```
chapter_10/client/echo_client/ios$ bazel build --apple_platform_type=ios
:Lib
INFO: Build option --apple_platform_type has changed, discarding analysis
cache.
INFO: Analyzed target //client/echo_client/ios:Lib (3 packages loaded,
     854 targets configured).
INFO: Found 1 target...
Target //client/echo_client/ios:Lib up-to-date:
  bazel-bin/client/echo_client/ios/Lib-Swift.h
  bazel-bin/client/echo_client/ios/client_echo_client_ios_Lib.swiftdoc
  bazel-bin/client/echo_client/ios/client_echo_client_ios_Lib.swiftmodule
  bazel-bin/client/echo_client/ios/libLib.a
```

```
INFO: Elapsed time: 4.139s, Critical Path: 3.72s
INFO: 2 processes: 1 darwin-sandbox, 1 worker.
INFO: Build completed successfully, 3 total actions
```

Having fully specified the platform, the build succeeds.

Note   You might recall from the prior chapter that we did not have to contend with specifying a platform explicitly. In the prior chapter, we used the rules android_ binary and android_library; like ios_application, these were sufficient for specifying the targets' build platform.

Note   Once again, an astute reader will notice the first INFO message, stating that the "analysis cache" has been discarded with the change in the build option. Recall that Bazel does a great deal of work to ensure the integrity of the build. In order to make sure that errors do not creep into the system, it is necessary to index the build products not only by *what* was built but also *how* it was built. Building a target with different options (e.g., platform, debug vs. opt, etc.) is basically equivalent to making a change to the target *and* all of its dependencies, at least for the purposes of caching the results.

Running the iOS Client in the Xcode Simulator

As we did for Android, we will take our initial build and run it on an iOS simulator to verify that it works.

We will first set up an iPhone simulator instance. Open Xcode, and navigate to *Xcode ➤ Open Developer Tool ➤ Simulator*.

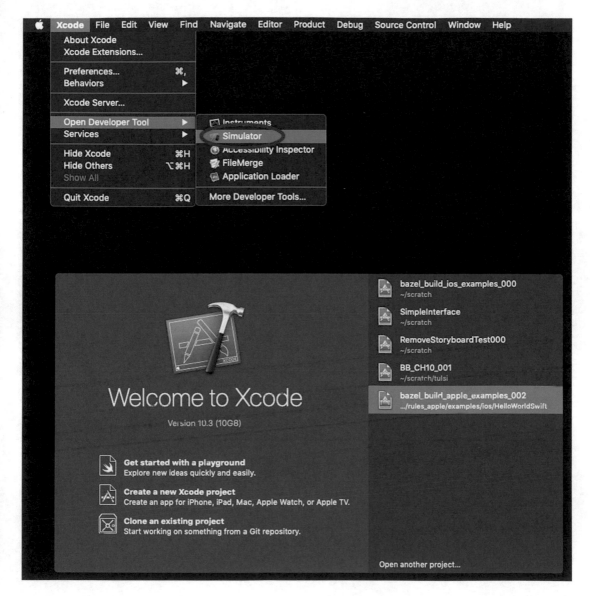

Figure 10-1. *Starting the Simulator*

Having started Simulator, you can now close down Xcode (this is similar to what we did in the last chapter with Android Studio).

In the Simulator application, let's create a hardware device for an iPhone Xs with iOS 12.4.

Figure 10-2. *Selecting a Particular iOS Device to Simulate*

This should create an instance of the iPhone Xs device simulator.

Figure 10-3. *iOS Simulator on Startup, for the Particular Device*

You are now ready to run the application on the simulator.

Executing the App on the Xcode Simulator

In the prior chapter, we were able to use bazel mobile-install <android_target>
in order to build and install our application directly onto an Android simulator.
Unfortunately, mobile-install only works for Android simulator instances; we can't use
exactly the same procedure for our iOS project. Attempting to do so would *build* but not
actually *execute* the target on the simulator.

We can approximate the same effect of the `mobile-install` by using some Xcode commands directly. First, let's make sure the build target is completely up to date. We will take particular note of the location of the generated .ipa file:

```
chapter_10/client/echo_client/ios$ bazel build :EchoClient
Starting local Bazel server and connecting to it...
INFO: Analyzed target //client/echo_client/ios:EchoClient (44 packages
      loaded, 1155 targets configured).
INFO: Found 1 target...
INFO: Deleting stale sandbox base /private/var/tmp/_bazel_pj/6ba16646dc915b
      8e018ad2c967b485b8/sandbox
Target //client/echo_client/ios:EchoClient up-to-date:
  bazel-bin/client/echo_client/ios/EchoClient.ipa
INFO: Elapsed time: 12.762s, Critical Path: 0.39s
INFO: 0 processes.
INFO: Build completed successfully, 1 total action
```

The .ipa file is actually a zipped directory. Although we cannot directly install the .ipa file onto the simulator, we can unzip it and install the underlying .app directory onto the simulator. Let's first unzip the .ipa file to get its underlying contents:

```
chapter_10/client/echo_client/ios$ cd ../../..
chapter_10$ unzip bazel-bin/client/echo_client/ios/EchoClient.ipa
Archive:  bazel-bin/client/echo_client/ios/EchoClient.ipa
   creating: Payload/
   creating: Payload/EchoClient.app/
   creating: Payload/EchoClient.app/_CodeSignature/
 extracting: Payload/EchoClient.app/_CodeSignature/CodeResources
 extracting: Payload/EchoClient.app/EchoClient
   creating: Payload/EchoClient.app/Frameworks/
 extracting: Payload/EchoClient.app/Frameworks/libswiftCoreImage.dylib
 extracting: Payload/EchoClient.app/Frameworks/libswiftObjectiveC.dylib
 extracting: Payload/EchoClient.app/Frameworks/libswiftCore.dylib
 extracting: Payload/EchoClient.app/Frameworks/libswiftCoreGraphics.dylib
```

```
extracting: Payload/EchoClient.app/Frameworks/libswiftUIKit.dylib
extracting: Payload/EchoClient.app/Frameworks/libswiftMetal.dylib
extracting: Payload/EchoClient.app/Frameworks/libswiftDispatch.dylib
extracting: Payload/EchoClient.app/Frameworks/libswiftos.dylib
extracting: Payload/EchoClient.app/Frameworks/libswiftCoreFoundation.dylib
extracting: Payload/EchoClient.app/Frameworks/libswiftDarwin.dylib
extracting: Payload/EchoClient.app/Frameworks/libswiftQuartzCore.dylib
extracting: Payload/EchoClient.app/Frameworks/libswiftFoundation.dylib
extracting: Payload/EchoClient.app/Info.plist
extracting: Payload/EchoClient.app/PkgInfo
```

Next, we will identify the active instance of the Xcode simulator by executing the following command. We are looking for the ID of the active instance:

```
chapter_10$ xcrun simctl list | grep Booted
 iPhone Xs (1DE26879-2844-4036-ABE2-A6B718A9CADA) (Booted)
 Phone: iPhone Xs (1DE26879-2844-4036-ABE2-A6B718A9CADA) (Booted)
```

Although it appears that there are two active instances, a close inspection reveals that the IDs are identical. Now, we are ready to install the application on the simulator. Execute the following command:

```
chapter_10$ xcrun simctl install 1DE26879-2844-4036-ABE2-A6B718A9CADA
Payload/EchoClient.app
```

Within the application, you should see the following.

Figure 10-4. *Installed Application on the Simulator*

Click the EchoClient application. You should see the following.

Figure 10-5. *Running the iOS EchoClient*

For the basic application, you should also be able to tap on the input text box, write some text, and have it locally echo to the output label.

Figure 10-6. *Running a Simple Echo Test (Local only)*

Congratulations! You have created and installed your first iOS application using Bazel!

Adding the gRPC to the iOS Application

Finally, as you have done in prior chapters, let's add the gRPC functionality. As you might expect, the work required for iOS closely mimics what you did for the other clients.

Open proto/BUILD and add the following changes, highlighted in bold.

Listing 10-6. Adding in the Swift protobuf rules

```
load("@io_bazel_rules_go//proto:def.bzl", "go_proto_library")
load("@io_grpc_grpc_java//:java_grpc_library.bzl", "java_grpc_library")
load("@build_bazel_rules_swift//swift:swift.bzl", "swift_grpc_library",
"swift_proto_library")

proto_library(
    name = "transmission_object_proto",
    srcs = ["transmission_object.proto"],
)

<content omitted for brevity>

swift_proto_library(
    name = "transmission_object_swift_proto",
    deps = [":transmission_object_proto"],
    visibility = ["//client/echo_client:__subpackages__"],
)

swift_proto_library(
    name = "transceiver_swift_proto",
    deps = [":transceiver_proto"],
    visibility = ["//client/echo_client:__subpackages__"],
)

swift_grpc_library(
    name = "transceiver_swift_proto_grpc",
    srcs = [":transceiver_proto"],
    flavor = "client",
    deps = [":transceiver_swift_proto"],
    visibility = ["//client/echo_client:__subpackages__"],
)
```

Save the file to proto/BUILD. The addition of the swift_proto_library and swift_grpc_library rules should come as no surprise to you.

> **Note**   Both the `swift_proto_library` and the `swift_grpc_library` will auto-generate Swift module names as a combination of the path (relative to the root of the workspace) to the target and the target name itself. For example, in this case, the module name for `transmission_object_swift_proto`, whose relative path is `/proto`, will have a module name of `proto_transmission_object_swift_proto`.

Having created these new targets, let's add them into our iOS Application. Open the `client/echo_client/ios/BUILD` file and add the following changes, highlighted in bold.

Listing 10-7. Adding in the Swift protobuf dependencies

```
load("@build_bazel_rules_apple//apple:ios.bzl", "ios_application")
load("@build_bazel_rules_swift//swift:swift.bzl", "swift_library")

swift_library(
    name = "Lib",
    srcs = [
        "AppDelegate.swift",
        "MainViewController.swift",
    ],
    deps = [
        "//proto:transmission_object_swift_proto",
        "//proto:transceiver_swift_proto",
        "//proto:transceiver_swift_proto_grpc",
    ],
)

ios_application(
    name = "EchoClient",
    bundle_id = "com.beginning-bazel.echo-client",
    families = ["iphone"],
    infoplists = [":Info.plist"],
    minimum_os_version = "11.0",
    deps = [":Lib"],
)
```

Now, we will add the Swift code for actually performing the gRPC call. Open `client/echo_client/ios/MainViewController.swift` and add the following, highlighted in bold.

Listing 10-8. Adding in the send/receive functionality

```
import UIKit
import proto_transmission_object_proto
import proto_transceiver_proto
import proto_transceiver_swift_proto_grpc

 <omitted for brevity>

    @objc func send(sender: UIButton!) {
        let client = Transceiver_TransceiverServiceClient(address:
        "localhost:1234", secure: false)

        var transmissionObject = TransmissionObject_TransmissionObject()
        transmissionObject.message = textInput.text ?? ""
        transmissionObject.value = 3.14

        var request = Transceiver_EchoRequest()
        request.fromClient = transmissionObject

        let response = try? client.echo(request)
        if let response = response {
            receivedText.text = response.fromServer.textFormatString()
        }
    }
```

Save the changes to `client/echo_client/ios/MainViewController.swift`.

Note   You might note that, unlike what you configured for the Android Studio simulator, we have reverted to using "localhost" for the address of our server. This is the proper address for getting to your development machine from within the iOS simulator.

Having added the gRPC functionality, let's build and test our work:

```
chapter_10/client/echo_client/ios$ bazel build --apple_platform_type=ios
client/echo_client/ios:EchoClient
INFO: Analyzed target //client/echo_client/ios:EchoClient (16 packages
     loaded, 267 targets configured).
INFO: Found 1 target...
Target //client/echo_client/ios:EchoClient up-to-date:
  bazel-bin/client/echo_client/ios/EchoClient.ipa
INFO: Elapsed time: 1.851s, Critical Path: 0.09s
INFO: 0 processes.
INFO: Build completed successfully, 3 total actions
```

Note   An astute reader will notice that we have added the `--apple_platform_type=ios` directive to the command line. Earlier, the `ios_application` was sufficient to indicate how to compile `swift_library` target. In this case, since we are generating code for a protobuf dependency (which, as of this writing, might not yet properly handle the implicit toolchain transition), we explicitly specify the build option.

Having successfully built the app, let's get the newest version installed on the simulator, repeating our earlier steps (with first removing our earlier unzipped directory):

```
chapter_10/client/echo_client/ios$ cd ../../..
chapter_10/client/echo_client/ios$ rm -rf Payload
chapter_10$ unzip bazel-bin/client/echo_client/ios/EchoClient.ipa
chapter_10$ xcrun simctl install 1DE26879-2844-4036-ABE2-A6B718A9CADA
Payload/EchoClient.app
```

Open the newly installed app within the iOS simulator. Now let's run our server on the terminal:

```
chapter_10$ bazel run server/echo_server
Target //server/echo_server:echo_server up-to-date:
  bazel-bin/server/echo_server/darwin_amd64_stripped/echo_server
INFO: Elapsed time: 14.009s, Critical Path: 12.36s
INFO: 324 processes: 324 darwin-sandbox.
```

```
INFO: Build completed successfully, 328 total actions
INFO: Build completed successfully, 328 total actions
2019/09/06 06:12:21 Spinning up the Echo Server in Go...
```

When you enter in the text within the iOS simulator and click *Send*, you should get a familiar response in the output.

Figure 10-7. *Running the Echo Test Using gRPC*

Congratulations! You have successfully created an iOS application using Bazel, using gRPC to communicate.

Final Word

Throughout the course of this chapter, you expanded your Bazel knowledge for building applications for iOS. As you imagine, it would be very easy to build other applications for the MacOS family. As we saw in prior chapters, the given gRPC example is very much a toy example; however, it could be easily augmented to become vastly more interesting (e.g., a messaging application).

Index

A

Android Debug Bridge (ADB)
 commands, 153
Android platform
 Android Studio, 137
 client command, 160–162
 client option
  AndroidManifest.xml, 149
  attributes, 150
  binary, 151
  BUILD file, 149
  directory, 146
  EchoClientMainActivity.java file, 146
  emulator instance, 151, 152
  layout file, 148
  mobile installation, 153–155
 Emulator
  AVD Manager, 142
  completion window, 146
  creation, 141
  hardware screen, 143
  particular version, 144
  virtual device, 143
 environment, 137–139
 gRPC, 155–161
  AndroidManifest.xml file, 155
  dependencies, 158
  EchoClientMainActivity.java, 157
  modification, 156
 SDK Manager up and running, 139–141

 setup, 135
 version selection, 140
 WORKSPACE file, 135, 136

B

Bazel build system
 coherent and optimized method, 5
 dependency analysis, 4
 execution and caching, 4
 explicit dependency declaration, 3
 features of, 2
 high-level build language, 3
 installation instructions, 7
 meaning, 1
 microservices and mobile
  applications, 5
 situations, 6
 visibility features, 4
 workspace management, 4

C, D

Client/server program,
 WORKSPACE file, 57–58
Code organization
 BUILD file, 98
 client and server code
  build target, 110
  echo_server code, 108, 109
  protobuf code, 108

189

X, Y, Z